Published by CMI Books division of Z Squared Media, LLC, Cleveland Ohio.
No part of this publication may be reproduced, stored in a retrieval system, or transmitted in any form or by any means, electronic, mechanical, photocopying, recording, scanning, or otherwise, except as permitted under section 107 or 108 of the 1976 United States Copyright Act, without the prior written permission of the publisher.

ISBN 978-0-983-3307-1-4
Printed in the United States of America.

Managing Content Marketing

The Real-World Guide for Creating
Passionate Subscribers to Your Brand

By Robert Rose and Joe Pulizzi • Foreword by Jeff Hayzlett

Table of Contents

Foreword

The chief advertising officer is dead. Long live the chief content officer.

The marketing landscape is evolving in new and exciting ways. We no longer talk about ad campaigns. We talk about our value proposition, a meaningful relationship, and crafting an experience for our customers. As marketers, we have new opportunities to reach our customers everywhere we look. Video and mobile and social media are exploding at unpredictable rates, causing businesses to shift their focus and restructure their budgets.

As we identify new audiences, channels, and communities, we also discover brand new opportunities to interact, listen, get feedback, and respond. This is our new marketing landscape.

We must, in turn, transform our marketing strategy to match that landscape. That's easy to say, but much harder for businesses — and their marketers — to do. We need a roadmap to get us there.

We need goals, a plan, and a strategy. We need to re-evaluate and constantly answer the hard questions. We must make sure we fog the mirror and our business breathes. After all, just because you kill the cow doesn't mean you'll have steak for dinner.

Managing Content Marketing: The Real-World Guide for Creating Passionate Subscribers to Your Brand provides the vital steps required to navigate this new path called content marketing.

"Conditions of satisfaction" is business-speak for the criteria used to measure the outcome of a plan or project. Once well-defined, they help you gauge and monitor progress and ultimately measure your outcomes and success. For me, personally, three basic conditions of satisfaction underlie everything I do:

- Grow professionally
- Grow wealth
- Have fun

If I can't accomplish these things, I don't do it. Your own conditions of satisfaction may be very different, but they will still be fundamental to building a business case for content marketing. That is, once you "understand who YOU are" (what is your story?), this book outlines the process for the next step, which is "understand who THEY are" (why your customers should care about your story and how to make it stick).

Understanding "who THEY are" is critical to creating relevant and meaningful content. You need to know your customers better than your spouse or your best friend. What do they like? What do they do? What are their activities and hobbies? What products do they use? What do they read? What are they saying and when are they saying it?

All this creates the need for content — specifically content as part of a marketing strategy. Robert and Joe nail it when they say marketers are looking at all these new channels and building their business cases — if they even get that far — then filling the gap with content. How you build content and the message is as important, if not more important, than any step in the process.

It's all about the "step and repeat process." When creating marketing programs of any scale, every piece of content you create, every strategy, every element of everything you do should be thought of as "make ready" — something that can be used over and over, and in new ways to truly make an impact on customers. Step and repeat; one step, repeated over and over. This process gives you the best opportunity to leverage what you have by ensuring your efforts are always multiplied. You don't need zeroes for all the processes; you just need to keep doing more with what you have. This book does that. It lays out the road map and creates a fail-safe process for content marketing.

What gets me fired up about this book is that these guys have it so right — there's nothing new about content marketing; it's the evolution of opportunities around it that will propel us forward. No one ever died (that I know of) as the result of a marketing campaign. Take a risk! Step out on the edge! Be the chief content officer. Read on to find out how to implement, maintain, and measure your content marketing strategy.

Saddle up, marketers! Get ready for a transformational journey into your content marketing strategy.

Happy reading,
Jeffrey Hayzlett

Jeffrey Hayzlett is the bestselling author of The Mirror Test: Is Your Business Really Breathing? He is a global business celebrity as well as a content marketing cowboy. You can find him online at www.Hayzlett.com.

Introduction

Okay, you've opened the book. Thank you. Now it's our job to keep you engaged.

Marketing has changed. Past tense. By opening this book, you already know that. Now it's time to actually do something about it.

The sea change that has been talked about in the hundreds of marketing books that precede this one is well under way. We're all in agreement that the influences of the explosive growth of the mobile and social Web are creating seismic shifts in all areas of business. We watch, as the Web threatens the existence of entire content-oriented sectors such as periodicals, newspapers, book stores, record companies, and broadcast television. Others, such as software companies, financial services, healthcare, and advertising services are undergoing fundamental changes as the social and mobile Web matures, and "the cloud" offers more value. Entire job categories — such as HR benefits manager, travel agent, librarian, journalist, photographer, videographer, and Web designer — are going the way of the linotypist, stenographer, and elevator operator.

And this pace of change is quickening. In 2004, former U.S. Education Secretary Richard Riley was quoted as saying that "none of the top 10 jobs that will exist in 2010 exist today." This may possibly be the first time in history when college graduates are taking jobs in categories that didn't even exist when they first entered school. And today we know we are preparing our kids for occupations that haven't even been created yet.

But perhaps no function in the business organization has been as fundamentally revolutionized as marketing. The social and mobile Web has completely changed the speed, efficiency, and ease with which consumers can engage with each other and has had a tremendous impact on brands. This new engagement of the consumer — with keen awareness of their relationships and emerging social networks — now correlates to every single aspect of our business. Marketing now influences how our accountants account, researchers research, developers develop, service people service, and even how leaders lead.

Jeremiah Owyang, a former Forrester analyst now with the Altimeter Group, talked with *CRM Magazine* in April 2009 about the growth of the social Web and its effect. He said:

"The community will take charge. Social networking will only continue to facilitate the power shift toward the consumer."

So, yes, marketing has changed. The question is what are we going to do about it?

Content and Subscription: The New Marketing Opportunity

As growth of the social and mobile Web changes the methods of communication, the old lines of hierarchical relationships between business and consumer blur substantially. As consumers publish and share their opinions (both good and bad) with increasing ease, they can become more persuasive than even the company's voice itself. As Charlene Li and Josh Bernoff say in their book *Groundswell: Winning in a World Transformed by Social Technologies:*

"...people on the Internet showed they were in charge. Any individual can be stopped, co-opted, bought off, or sued. But the Internet allows people to draw strength from each other."

Every one of these groups becomes a powerful ally or enemy depending on what we do. All of them will be constantly in flux — developing levels of trust and requiring varying levels of transparency to filter content and determine buying decisions. They will expand and collapse with great velocity, and it will all happen with or without our participation. Seth Godin discusses this at length in his book *Tribes: We Need You to Lead Us.* According to Godin:

"Everyone is not just a marketer — everyone is now also a leader. The explosion in tribes, groups, covens, and circles of interest means that anyone who wants to make a difference can."

It's up to us as marketing managers to create, lead, and build loyalty among these groups so they work optimally for our business. This isn't manipulation, and it's not a "Lord-Of-The-Flies-like" capricious takeover of power just to ensure our survival. Whether it's called a "flattened earth" by Thomas Friedman ... "acquiring 1,000 fans" by

Kevin Kelly ... "building a tribe" by Godin ... or developing your "fanatics" by Guy Kawasaki ... the idea is that technology has empowered people to access markets much more efficiently. And new tools, including the Web, have made the relationship between buyer and seller much more fluid. Therefore, markets are much more competitive and transparent, and provide for much greater opportunity.

So our job is to lead these groups — and build loyalty.

At the heart of this leadership and loyalty strategy is one thing — content marketing. To succeed today, we need to use content to continually engage our audiences — from the first time we meet them, continuing throughout the entire customer lifecycle. In short, the job of marketing is no longer to create customers, it is (to paraphrase Peter Drucker) to create passionate subscribers to our brand.

Subscribers might seem like a funny word to describe what we're trying to create. But, Joe and co-author Newt Barrett described this well in their seminal book on content marketing *Get Content Get Customers*. They explained the opportunity this way:

"Marketing organizations are now realizing that they can create content whose quality is equal to or better than what many media companies are producing. Moreover, they are seeing that they can deliver tangible benefits to prospects and customers by offering relevant content that helps produce solutions to some of the toughest problems their prospective buyers are facing.

"By delivering content that is vital and relevant to your target market, you will begin to take on an important role in your customers' lives. This applies to your online, print, and in-person communications. And this is the same role that newspapers, magazines, TV, radio, conferences, workshops, and Web sites have played in the past. Now it's time for your organization to play that role."

A Seismic Shift

So, how do we approach this new content-driven marketing strategy? How does this affect the traditional marketing strategy function within our organization? How do we establish new processes in our organization to build and service our subscribers?

This newest evolution is having a huge effect on all aspects of our business. Whether it's building a subscriber base of evangelists (formerly known as customers) who will engage with our brand and talk about our product, or building a subscriber base around prospective customers so that we can nurture them into becoming customers (formerly known as leads) — the driver of building conversation about, as well as loyalty to, our brand will be one thing — content.

A content-as-marketing strategy will take many forms. The simplest, of course, is your current Web site, catalogs, and newsletters. According to a recent study conducted by the Content Marketing Institute and MarketingProfs, 9 out of 10 marketers are using content in some manner. However, there still remains a confidence gap in its effectiveness. Many marketers are creating lots of content but, for the most part, are unsure of its effectiveness and role within the organization.

On the other hand, we have a large percentage of marketers who are still trying to build a business case for content marketing, and when they do, find themselves trying to fill the gap to produce the content they need. In short, content creation is alive and well across most organizations, but the practice of content marketing — a repeatable strategic process — has been missing.

Content marketing is a strategy focused on the creation of a valuable experience. It is humans being helpful to each other, sharing valuable pieces of content that enrich the community and position the business as a leader in the field. It is content that is engaging, imminently sharable, and, most of all, focused on helping customers to discover (on their own) that your product or service is the one that will scratch their itch.

This "many to many" engagement strategy is a new muscle for most organizations — we have been in the business of "talking" through one "voice" for years. We've never before had to "listen" as deeply and react as quickly as we do today. Marketing has been thrust into the lead role here. Is it any wonder that marketing's role has expanded so exponentially — from not only building awareness and nurturing leads, but to servicing and engaging customers after the sale? And, today, even if we don't control it, content is flying in and out of our businesses. We have customers rating our products and services on social Web sites. We have product managers posting their opinions on LinkedIn, the CEO wanting to blog, and every salesperson in the company with his or her own Twitter account.

Simultaneously, as we read articles and books and watch experts at conferences extol the virtues of content marketing, we have to actually build a governed process that will help our business. No one told us in school that to be successful marketers we were going to have to become publishers. But this is what we're becoming. And, we have to find some way to effectively measure all this to know what's successful. Oh, and by the way — it's all shifting as we have to continue to provide results this quarter. It can just be plain overwhelming to many. Is it any wonder that so many marketers feel like their strategy is in crisis?

Well it is. Marketing is in a crisis!

The Rest of this Book

There is an ancient Chinese proverb that says a "crisis" is simply an "opportunity riding the dangerous wind." As marketers we now have the opportunity to develop new processes with our marketing strategy, power them with content, and ultimately keep that wind at our back.

Successful programs will focus on creating a thoughtful strategy and process to foster this content marketing. The rest of this book is a detailed "how-to" to build that successful process. There are five key points to understand before you can successfully accomplish this:

1. Understand who YOU are.

What is your organization poised to accomplish? What are the differentiating factors of your product or service? Who are the unique YOUs that differentiate your business? What is your organization best at providing?

2. Understand who THEY are.

Who and where are the communities you're serving? Have you been neglecting them for so long that they have grown roots in other places — or are they gathering around your brand in different ways? Who are the personas that make up the variety of communities? What are they passionate about? Who are their leaders? How can you reach them? If communities don't exist yet, how can you encourage them to form?

3. What CONTENT can you provide to them to build loyalty?

What is your story and how do you tell it? This goes beyond just an editorial calendar. How do you create compelling stories that feed your communities and generate passionate followings? Do you need to provide tools to facilitate communities, or just the content to foster them? What are your communities most interested in? What knowledge could you provide that would facilitate a natural tendency to want to buy from your business? (This is where you need to strategize the difference between content that is merely helpful, content that facilitates discussion, and content that is created with the explicit purpose to lead to a sale.)

4. Subscribers must be fed, nurtured, and yes — unsubscribed when it's time.

Communities are fluid. They naturally grow, shrink, merge, and disband. Pay close attention to how they are changing — continually monitoring them is what leads to success.

5. We can measure success.

Develop a process to measure success of how you service your loyal subscribers. There are various ways to accomplish this; most depend on what the servicing is and for what community. For example, if it is a sales-driven content marketing strategy, you might measure lead lift according to setting up registrations for the content. Or, if it's a customer service content marketing strategy, you could measure the decrease in customer service calls vs. the traffic in the engagement community.

The important thing to understand is you're not too late. Content marketing has been around for hundreds of years. John Deere's *Furrow Magazine* — devoted to teaching farmers best practices — has been around since 1895. But the application of a specific strategic process around content marketing is still new. Sure you're creating lots of content, but the *function* of content marketing probably doesn't even exist in your organization yet — or if it does, you may not even be calling it "content marketing." You need to be okay with that. The amount of budget that is allotted for new content creation is going to become a significant part of your "new media" budget. And subject matter experts in the organization are going to have new responsibilities. It's a transformative new process — and it won't happen overnight. But it can, and should, happen. *Get Content Get Customers* showed us the light — but there's been no book to show us the way.

Until now ...

PART ONE
CONTENT MARKETING
STRATEGY

Chapter 1
Build the Business Case

"Due to budget cuts, the light at the end of the tunnel has been turned off."

—a sign in Boston, 2008

One of the most frustrating things about being at a marketing conference is that you'll see session after session of pundits talking about the new, next thing — and imploring you to "build the business case for it." Of course, they never tell you HOW to build the business case for it — but nevertheless you should do as they say.

Content marketing is no exception to this rule. Without doubt, the question we get asked most is, "How do I build a business case?"

While the practice of content marketing is certainly not new — making it a formal, budgeted process in your organization is. And that's an important point. It has the potential to be an innovative new piece to your marketing mix. And it's where you, as marketers, have to become hungry for innovation.

So before you even start to build a tactical "business case" for content marketing, you have to build a business case for innovation. That sounds simple enough, but we know that some of you struggle to get anything "new" into your organization at all — much less something like content marketing.

Here's a fun exercise. Walk around your office and ask everybody three questions. The first one is: "Should companies be innovative?" We'll take a wild guess and predict a 90%+ response in the affirmative.

Then, independent of the answer, immediately ask the next one: *"Has our company ever been innovative?"* Here, you may get that confused 4 p.m. I Haven't Had My Snickers Bar look. They may ask, *"Do you mean are we innovative right now?"* And, you'll reply *"no — I'm asking have we ever been innovative? Ever?"*

Of those who say *"yes, we've been innovative,"* you can bet that every one of them will cite a success when you ask the third and final question: *"When?"*

See — everybody LOVES innovation — you know, just so long as it worked.

Nobody wants to be the dopey person who said "yes" to the new product that sold five units. As a friend said recently, "I'd rather get a zero on a test than a 22, because a 22 means I tried."

Build the Business Case for Innovation

It seems like a silly question — and maybe in your business it's unrelated to building the business case for content marketing. But it's often not. Building the business case for innovation is a huge piece of starting to introduce an innovative process like content marketing into an organization. Why? Because it's quite simply getting permission to fail. There's no way to prove return on investment (ROI) before you innovate, because by definition it hasn't been proven before. In order to build more innovative and disruptive successes in your marketing, you have to have the capability to tolerate more failure.

Here are some ideas you can put into place to start to introduce these concepts into your organization:

Build Small, Adaptive Experiments Separate from the Core

Allow a small experimental team or effort that can operate outside the bounds of your traditional measurement schemes. A skunkworks? Yes, but by whatever name, dedicate a small percentage of your budget to fund these efforts — and make it a point to NOT measure it against traditional factors. EVERY single thing done in this area should have permission to fail. Maybe it's just one or two things — but let it be innovative, and truly new.

This puts a little more pressure on your budget (we know). But try this out. Make a promise to your boss/CEO/CFO. For every $1 you save through marketing efficiency (and we're about to show you exactly that), tell them you want to put half into an innovation fund. Point out that 20% of every Google employee's time goes into just this kind of innovation, and all you are looking for is to spend what you save.

Generate New Types of Networking Groups for Innovation
There's a wonderful book called *Open Innovation: Researching a New Paradigm* by Henry Chesbrough. In it, he and his editors discuss the idea of designing innovation through both internal AND external sources. Consider setting up a group of people you don't otherwise communicate with and generating new marketing ideas. The IT guy in the corner might just have a good idea.

Build an Actual Innovation Business Plan and Share It
This one seems a bit counterintuitive, but building a structured process for innovation is more than gathering a new group in a conference room and throwing sticky notes up on a wall (although that's fun). Consider building a structure and plan for your innovation. The contents of this plan should be:

- **The Challenge?** — What challenges are you trying to solve?

- **The Ultimate Outcome** — What is your dream outcome of this process?

- **The Risk** — What's the risk if you fail?

- **Who's Involved** — Whose unique perspective do you want here? If internal, what permission do you need from their managers to participate?

- **The Budget** — How much will you spend on this endeavor?

- **Deliverables** — What are you shooting for? One new idea per month? One experiment per week? (Yes, we know this is hard to determine, but setting goals is the only way to measure any progress.)

- **The Big Red "Oh Shit" Button** — If life or business issues get in the way, how can you push a big red button without disbanding the whole idea of the innovation business plan? How can you mitigate the damage that a missed quarter, an unexpected client departure, or a cut in marketing might cause?

- **Action Plans** — How will you execute each experimental idea and how long will you give it to work or not? (Develop a template for this so you don't have to format each plan.)

In the end, the reality is that you may or may not get "permission" to do this in your organization.

But, here's the thing. If you try — and succeed — you will start crafting a job that is about so much more than just incrementally decreasing costs in marketing spend and managing a budget. And if you try — and you fail — well … guess what? You will have innovated.

That leads us into creating a culture that's ripe for implementing an innovative process like content marketing. And, here, at some point — regardless of your culture — you will need to build a business case for how content marketing will work in your organization. As part of your innovation plan, it might be just one small test. Or, you might really believe your content strategy will work and you need a case to move a great percentage of next year's budget into it. Maybe you're looking for internal rationalization for the business you own — or maybe you need to convince a stonewalling CFO in the giant corporation you work for. Whatever the case, you have some work on your hands.

Build the Business Case for Content Marketing

At its surface, this can seem like a particularly daunting challenge. Content marketing is so new for most organizations — and tends to involve so many different parts of the business — that it's often difficult to identify the "hard benefits" or "numbers" that are going to really drive the business value.

Let's start at the beginning — and look step-by-step at how we might build the business case.

Like any good business plan, the business case for content marketing answers five questions succinctly:

1. What's the need?

What do you hope to accomplish with your content marketing?

2. How big of a need is it?

Is the need big enough to build an entire plan around?

3. What's the business model?

How does it work? What do you have to do?

4. What's your differentiating value?

Why is this initiative more important than other things you're spending resources on?

5. What are the risks?

What's in your way of success — or what happens if you fail?

Do you notice what's NOT in there? That's right — it's the thing that almost everybody starts off with: *"how much is this going to cost?"* And next — *"how much are we going to get back?"*

Let's be clear about something: A business case is not ROI. Too many times, we see marketing organizations try to apply an ROI on content marketing as if it were a media tactic like a banner advertisement or an email campaign. Trying to pin ROI on content marketing is a bit like asking "what's the ROI on your telephone system?"

ROI is not the metric that should be used to determine whether content marketing is worth doing. The ROI is a GOAL or OBJECTIVE, specific to the desired result, which we set within the business case.

For example, if a salesperson fails to provide a positive return on an outbound telephone campaign, you don't conclude that the telephone system is failing to provide ROI. You look at the specific actions (e.g., the salesperson's skills, the message they used, and the prospect call list) and determine which action failed to provide the expected ROI. You make adjustments and adapt.

For content marketing, the expected "return" may be part of #2 above (defining the size of the opportunity) — and certainly, your expected "investment" is part of #3 (defining the level of effort). But these are only definitions — they should not be determining factors as to whether or not you proceed.

Here are a few examples of ROI that you might define in your content marketing strategy:

- **Tracking sales lift** among those who receive the content marketing initiative vs. those who do not.

- **Tracking conversions** for online content products or print subscriptions and measuring new or increased sales.

- **Measuring engagement** — time spent on your site or content programs to see how that's equating to a higher engagement level for the audiences you're targeting.

- **Pre/post awareness** to measure the impact of the program.

This point bears repeating (just in case you don't go up and reread the above) — the ROI equation is NOT the business case. ROI measurements are goals you set once you've put the business case into action. We'll look more closely at ROI and how we measure success against our business case in Chapter 2.

For now, let's take a look at each piece of the business case separately.

1. What's the need?

Unless you can visualize what success looks like, there's not much sense in even starting to build a case for it. What are you trying to accomplish? Every business has a version of the sales funnel. Your sales funnel may be labeled differently — or it may have different conversion metrics (or more or less of them). But generally they start at some level of awareness — and through your process, consumers move down the funnel through conversion layers (or sales cycles) until they become customers.

Customers   Customers

The sales funnel.

Now here's where it gets interesting. Because content marketing is useful beyond the customer stage — it can be used as an upsell or reinforcement mechanism ... to build customer satisfaction ... or even to develop community to start building brand subscribers — we need a new way to look at the funnel.

The Content Marketing Funnel

With content marketing, there are a number of overall business goals you could have. Using the content marketing funnel as an example, let's identify which make the most sense for your particular initiative:

Brand awareness or reinforcement.
This is almost always the first thing that is thought of when you look at content marketing. The goal may be that you are just trying to find a more effective way than advertising to create awareness for your product or service. This is the "long tail" strategy. Content marketing is a great vehicle for that, as it's organic, authentic, and a great way for you to start driving engagement with your brand.

Lead conversion and nurturing.

The most basic part of inbound marketing is the conversion metric. How you define a lead will vary — but from a content marketing perspective, this is where you have (through the exchange of engaging content) encouraged someone to give up enough information about themselves that you now have permission to "market" to them. This can include signing up for a "demo," registering for an event, subscribing to your e-newsletter, or gaining access to your Resource Center. Once you have the prospect's permission, you can use content to help move them through the buying cycle.

Customer conversion.

In many cases, you already have a ton of content in this area. This is where, as marketers, we have traditionally focused — the "proof points" to the sale. Examples include case studies you send to your prospects that illustrate how you've solved the problem before — or the "testimonials" section on your client page. Ultimately, this is the content you've created as a marketer to illustrate to the hot prospect why your solution is better or will uniquely meet his or her need.

Customer service.

This is where content marketing can really earn its "subscribe" stripes. How well are you using content to create value or reinforce the customer's decision AFTER the sale? This goes well beyond the user manual, the documented process for success, and the FAQ on your Web site. These are the best practices for how to use your product or service. How can customers get the MOST out of your product or service? What are the successful, innovative ways that you've seen your product or service get extended into other solutions?

Customer upsell.

Marketing doesn't stop at the "checkout" button any longer. If you're particularly good at using content to service the customer in a subscribe model, you also have the opportunity to be effective at creating ongoing engagement for the other products and services you offer. Why stop communicating with prospects once they become customers? Instead, communicate with them more frequently (certainly not in a creepy way) and engage them with additional value.

Passionate subscribers.

If you can successfully move customers to this stage, you have really accomplished something. Content — and especially content generated by satisfied customers — can be one of the most powerful ways for us to reach any business goal. This is when content marketing starts to work for you exponentially. Apple Computer is the quintessential example of this. Ask yourself what their content marketing strategy is. They have no social media presence. They have no blog. But they have successfully built their passionate subscriber base — and these people create fan sites, write, share, and evangelize the Apple® brand. Your ultimate goal should be to create a community of evangelists who are prepared to fight for your brand.

So which of these goals makes sense for your content marketing? Maybe it's a limited initiative and you're just trying to help drive more leads into the sales and marketing process. Maybe you're trying to create a program that increases awareness, drives down the cost of organic traffic to your Web site, and increases your position with search engines. Take a moment now to get your mental juices flowing. What do you want to accomplish with content marketing?

2. How big of an opportunity is it?

Once you've defined your opportunity and where you want to focus your efforts (at least initially), the next step is to identify how big the opportunity is. Is it substantial enough to justify your efforts?

Remember back in college when you learned about TAM (the Total Addressable Market)? For those of you who were "sick" that day (and here's where we put on our professor glasses for a moment), the TAM is used to identify the "revenue opportunity" that is available for your new product or service. You basically estimate how much of a particular market you could gain with your new product or service, were there no competition. For example, if you were marketing a new, fancy dog collar, you would look at the number of "dog owners" in the market you were trying to address. That number — multiplied by the price of your dog collar — would be your TAM.

Okay, taking off the professor glasses — your content marketing opportunity is similar. You need to ask yourself, "what effect can we optimally create — given no impediments?"

Here are three simple steps for determining the size of the opportunity:

Know your targets.

One of the keys to understanding whether a content marketing strategy will work is really understanding who your target markets are and how you are servicing them. One of the most common mistakes is creating a content marketing strategy from the inside out. We look at our "library" of content and then spray it out broadly like an unfocused broadcast TV network. Instead, we need to think more like cable television. We need to focus specific content to specific target audiences.

To develop your business case, and define your opportunity, you need to understand who your target "subscriber" is — and what the impact will be if you make a difference. In other words — in order for content marketing to have impact — you need to know WHO it will have impact on — and, ultimately, how much potential that impact will have on your business.

Feel their pain.

Let's face it — if our business is printing money and our customers are over-the-moon-happy with us — then we probably don't need content marketing. If that's true for you, what the heck are you doing reading this book? In fact, we'd rather read yours.

The reality is that content marketing is an enhancement to your current marketing efforts and you need to understand what gap you are trying to fill. Okay, so you know your target market and you understand the potential impact of serving them with better content. But what does "serving better" mean? That's what you want to understand.

Here's an example: Let's say your current customer base is made up of 80% men and 20% women — but your product is equally appropriate for both sexes. Clearly, you're not attracting enough women. Maybe there's a content marketing program you could put in place to target the LARGE universe of women that could be — but for some reason are not — attracted to your product. In order to "feel their pain," you should identify the need you want to satisfy with content. A great example of this is Procter & Gamble's HomeMadeSimple.com Web site. P&G uses the site as an informational portal to attract "moms" to various brands, then separately uses ManOfTheHouse.com to target "dads" for the same types of products.

What's the BIG idea?

How will this large opportunity translate into big success? What happens if you successfully meet the initial goals you set? What happens if you successfully ease the pain that the target group is feeling?

Here we begin to see the opportunity for RETURN on investment. This is where we bring in the numbers and talk about how many MORE sales, or what REDUCTION in costs we'll have if we're successful.

This exercise to determine the size of the opportunity is fundamentally about answering three questions:

- Can we use content marketing to ease an existing pain or to enhance our existing marketing successfully?
- Is this opportunity big enough to warrant spending our time and/or money on?
- Assuming the answers to #1 and #2 are "yes," then the final question is "by how much?"

Which brings us to our next step.

3. What's the business model?

Now that you've identified the goal — and how much impact it can have on your business — you have to face reality and understand what it will actually take to get there.

Let's be brutally honest. This is the part of the business case that most people want to skip. This is the part where we should define ALL the things that will need to happen in order for us to be successful.

And, quite frankly, this is where developing a content marketing business case can get a bit overwhelming. Content marketing is almost assuredly just one thing of hundreds that you're dealing with in your business. I mean, let's face it, you're just never going to have enough time, patience, or budget to do the type of process modeling that "guarantees" risk-free operations. So, the key with defining the model of how you will operationalize the content marketing to meet the stated goals is to identify only WHAT YOU NEED to successfully make your case.

What does that mean? Well it means that you need to identify what the process is going to look like — and how that will affect the rest of the business. And it means that you need to do so in ONLY the detail absolutely necessary for you to move forward.

The amount of documentation and detail will obviously be unique to your business, and the person you're trying to convince. If it's just YOU — then a gut feeling here may be sufficient. If it's the CFO at a Fortune 500 company, we're going to bet you'll need a bit more detailed analysis. Keep in mind that the more detailed operational process may come out of the strategy that is yet to be developed; however, in general, your model should focus on these three things:

1. What is the SCOPE of your initial content marketing plan?
2. What is the team you will need to address that scope?
3. How will this affect your existing marketing efforts?

Remember, as you frame this initiative, it is a process that you are embarking on — not a project. The operational process that you design will change significantly as you ramp up (or down) your efforts. It will change as your business changes, as technology changes, as the economy or marketing trends change. Just know that it will evolve.

For all of these reasons — while you are looking to include some general projections of staffing and levels of effort and expense — these will change as your program develops successfully … or doesn't. But because you have already hypothesized your level of RETURN (you did that when you identified the opportunity, didn't you?) — you already have some line in the sand that you know you can't cross. Your confidence level in reaching this line should be reflected in your operational recommendation. This is where you start looking back at your earlier efforts in this process and ask yourself if you've gotten too aggressive with your initial estimates — or whether you're being too cautious.

You can also look ahead to the next step (below) and start to analyze your current efforts. These should help inform your business case. If you're looking for content marketing tactics to perform exponentially better than other things you're doing, you should have a much stronger operational case than if you're just looking for incremental improvement.

4. What's your differentiating value?

Now that you have a general idea of what your level of effort is going to be — and what your goal of return should be — you need to be able to illustrate what the differentiated value of your content marketing plan will be.

Take a look at the marketing you've being doing up to this point. How well has SEO done? Pay-per-click (PPC) advertising? Your "up-sell" efforts? Do you have a solid social media strategy — or none at all? All of these have metrics associated with them; analyze them to determine whether you might want to divert funds from some of these initiatives into your content marketing plan. Ask yourself which of your initiatives:

- Failed (e.g., didn't produce the desired results)
- Didn't support the marketing goals
- Worked well but are now finished — giving you the flexibility to move on to something new.

When you tie this information to your content marketing plan, you may be able to forecast some differentiated value. For example:

- We anticipate a 10% lift in PPC leads as a result of executing a content marketing plan.

- Defunding the corporate blog and redirecting the money to product-level blogs should give us more "quality" prospects.
- Shifting our budget from an outsourced SEO strategy to an internal content production process should increase our SEO over time.

See how each of those has a differentiating value? The first states that if we do this, we'll get 10% lift in our PPC efforts. That's an easy one to put a dollar figure on. The second states that we'd like to replace the budget for a defunded (ineffective) project with one that we believe will provide better leads. That one can have sales metrics associated with it. And the third states that now that we have accomplished the goal of getting an SEO-optimized site, we'd like to create a content marketing budget to reinforce and maintain that investment. In other words — we just spent XYZ on building a garden — we should create a budget for water and fertilizer.

While working on this part of your plan, make sure to cover these two important factors:

Ensure that each content marketing initiative is aligned to business objectives. Every piece of content should support a measurable marketing objective — whether that's increased awareness, increased opportunities, increased revenue, customer retention or customer satisfaction. Assign each content marketing process (item) to one of these measurable objectives. The more specific you can make these recommendations, the more likely you are building differentiating value. To put this into perspective for you, here are the main objectives that marketers stated from the recently released 2011 Content Marketing Institute/MarketingProfs B2B Content Marketing Research.

Organization's (or client's) Goals for Content Marketing

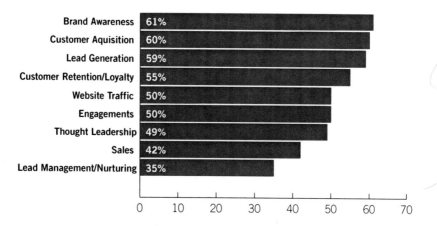

Goal	%
Brand Awareness	61%
Customer Aquisition	60%
Lead Generation	59%
Customer Retention/Loyalty	55%
Website Traffic	50%
Engagements	50%
Thought Leadership	49%
Sales	42%
Lead Management/Nurturing	35%

Organization's (or client's) goals for content marketing.

As you can see, most organizations are still focusing on brand awareness and customer acquisition as their main goals.

Then, once you've assigned specific marketing objectives — understand your company's marketing budget ratios and how they apply to your content.

There are a number of ways organizations measure marketing ratios, and many have different acronyms for this. However, most of them basically use this equation:

For every $1 of marketing spend, we get/expect $X of return in revenue.

Notice that there are two verbs there — "get" and "expect." You need to know both numbers.

For example, startup companies trying to grab market share will often have a ratio of 2 (or more) to 1. But at some point, unless the marketing team wants to get axed, that ratio needs to come down. In the end, this number might be around 15% (e.g., $1 marketing for every $6.50 in revenue) or, as with some service firms we've seen, as low as 1%. The key is to understand both what it "is" and what the CFO "expects" it to be — and by when.

Knowing both of these numbers can help you to create differentiated value for a new content marketing expenditure. So if that new thought leadership blog is going to cost $5K to get up and running and the CFO "expect" ratio is 15%, then you should be confident that the blog will ultimately produce about $35K of incremental revenue.

Bonus tip: If you understand the length of time it will take to get there, you'll get a gold star in your personnel file. Trust us, if you walk in and say — "I want to launch this new blog. It will cost $5K to launch — and I'm forecasting $35K of revenue sourced from it in six months" — you're going to get a big smile from the CFO.

But whoa, wait a minute. How do you know if your blog is actually going to create $35K worth of revenue? Well, you don't. Again, we're building a "business case," not a guarantee. Assuming that you've gone through all the previous steps, you should be confident that you can achieve this differentiated value. But every business plan has risk — and that's the point. You're not trying to prove ROI from the beginning, but rather building a business case against a risk that you can manage.

That's an extremely important factor and brings us to our second key to building differentiated value.

Budget for failure.

Remember your business case for innovation. As your initiatives get larger and more complex, make sure you not only budget at least a small percentage of content marketing spend for new experiments that may not work, but also set the expectation as well. Every good financial analyst understands the benefits of managing "low, medium, and high risk" efforts in a portfolio — and your content marketing budgets should be no different. They will change as you experience both success and failure — so making sure you budget for both is important.

As Joe recently said in a post on Junta42.com on how to manage the content marketing process:

"If the budget you created at the start of the year is not drastically different than the one you ended up with, you probably aren't listening enough to what your customers need."

Effectively communicating the differentiating value of what you're trying to accomplish to your team will ensure that you're not fighting for resources and always wondering if you can try something new. It also ensures that you'll continue to grow — even if your budget doesn't.

That brings us to the last piece of the business case.

5. What are the risks?

Risk is what makes our business interesting and challenging. If we were guaranteed to be successful at everything we did, what would be the point of doing it?

Marketing is one of the riskier parts of the business. There are so many parameters that can "go wrong" that it can be overwhelming to try and manage it. To create an effective business case, you should identify the risks — and what you can do to mitigate them should they arise. In your business case, be sure to:

1. Identify and evaluate the impacts and possible sources of the content marketing risk on achieving the goals you've set.

2. Focus on the things you can control — and identify what you can do to minimize the possibility of these things occurring.

3. If your risk mitigation plans will increase the costs and/or return you can achieve, identify those to the best of your ability.

Because this is a new process, you need to think about the potential risks and what you will do if they occur. For example, new processes often have new requirements from different departments. For instance, you may need to have your legal department review any new content you produce to ensure that you're not making claims or running afoul of any compliance guidelines. This may affect your ability to create content that truly resonates with your target audience. Or maybe you find that you need to bring in external partners, which may mean additional time or effort on your part.

Again, no good business case eliminates risk — but simply mitigates it, and provides a plan to manage it. The way to mitigate the risk in any process is to build in some "insurance." Identifying how you can suffer through a number of these risks and mitigate them illustrates that you've thought them through and strengthens your business case.

REAL LIFE EXAMPLE — Case Study
Camp Champions — Developing a Business Case for Content Marketing for the Social Web

If there's anyone who knows the value of a good "business case" it's Steve Baskin. The owner and CEO of Camp Champions, a boys and girls summer camp for children ages 6 to18, Steve started his professional life as an investment banker with Goldman Sachs in New York. He was responsible for managing millions of dollars of other people's money. After graduating from Harvard Business School, Steve decided to pursue his true passion: summer camp. He and his wife Susie (a graduate of Kellogg Business School at Northwestern University) have been full-time campers since 1993, and today operate one of the largest summer camps in the central Texas region.

We worked with Steve and his team of dedicated campers to develop a solid business case for content marketing — specifically targeting the social Web. Using the structure we've just outlined, let's look at how they did it.

1. What was their need?

Camp Champions is a successful camp for sure — they maintain great enrollment and year after year see increases in camper families. But challenging economic times have certainly put a financial strain on their constituents. Some parents, particularly parents that did not attend camp, view summer camp as a discretionary purchase. Parenting trends have made parents overly protective, even hovering as in the case of "helicopter parents." These trends, coupled with the expense of summer camp have made camp a much more demanding purchase for parents than ever before. Combine all this with the fact that some parents who send their child to camp are made to feel guilty by other parents as "outsourcing parenthood."

Camp Champion's need was twofold. First, Steve and Susie wanted to attract new "camp kids" by better leveraging their Web site and social Web presence (primarily Facebook). It certainly wasn't lost on them that more and more parents were using the Web and "referral" sites to make initial camp decisions.

The second goal was to help parents feel good about their decision to send their children to camp. Basically Camp Champion wanted to use content to help reinforce both the decision a new parent was about to make — and that an existing parent had already made so as to encourage them to continue to send their kid to camp for the next year. They wanted their parents to understand the youth development benefits of camp and to know that their children are loved. What great goals!

2. How big of a need was it?

By Camp Champions' estimate, the perfect scenario is for a family to send their child to camp for 10 years — from age 8 to 18. To put that into "marketing terms" — the Total Lifetime Value of each child is $25K to $30K. Adding even a handful of new campers each year — and reassuring an equal number of parents that they've made the right decision and continue to send their kids to camp — can equal tens of thousands of dollars of incremental revenue per year. Using these numbers, Camp Champions immediately knew how much effort they could put forth and measure. Now, more importantly, the pain that needed to be alleviated was that of justifying the cost. In a struggling economy, Camp Champions needed parents to understand that camp is more than a "luxury vacation" our "outsourced babysitting" for their child. By focusing their efforts on using content to convince and reassure parents that their child was benefitting developmentally by attending camp, they could address the goals they set forth.

3. What was their differentiating value?

One of the main efforts in the existing sales process for Camp Champions and their marketing efforts was the "open house" and the "information party." At these parties, kids are split off and get to enjoy the fun of camp while the parents are split off to learn about how camp is more than "fun" but also a huge developmental assistant. Using research, child experts, and the expertise Steve and Susie have developed with more than 19 years in the camp business, parents really get to understand that it's much more than just sending their kids to "babysitting" — it's about furthering their educational and personal development. This became the business model of their content marketing — they could then assemble a content strategy and process that made sense for their business, and use their Web site and social media to create a "permanent information party."

By looking at their opportunity and the monetary value of 1) what a new and/or saved parent would deliver them, 2) how many new customers they got from information parties, and 3) how much incremental effort would be required by staff to feed a content marketing plan, Camp Champions was able to see what the math looked like. They knew that these goals couldn't be supported by traditional advertising. The Web and social media made perfect sense for them. They set goals — and believed that by assigning efforts — they would see incremental results on those goals. And, by feeding everything through their Web site — where they already had metrics set up — they could measure the results.

4. What were the risks?

The risks they identified revolved around time. With a small staff, they would have to work hard to keep the content fresh and updated. They had to make time to find and analyze external research — and to make it approachable and relevant for the parents they served. And, because of their location in central Texas, they needed to decide whether translating this external content into Spanish for their International audiences made sense. Additionally, they recognized that using social Web channels created the risk that kids or parents might post unfavorable things about their experiences at camp. They identified these risks and came up with policies and guidelines for staff to deal with them should they arise.

In the end, with such a small team, the Camp Champions staff felt no need to codify any of this in any formal "business plan" document. It was simply a process — and thinking through all these things central-ized everybody's feelings about the worth of the content program. It gave Steve and Susie clarity about how their efforts should pay off — and what they should expect down the road. Time will tell if they execute the plan well — but they have built a content marketing business case that any CEO would be proud of.

Chapter 2
Who's on First and Why?

"All the people like us are We,
and everyone else is They."

—Rudyard Kipling

I n the book *Data Smog: Surviving the Information Glut,* author David Shenk says that in 1971 the average American was exposed to 560 advertising messages per day. By 1997, that number had increased to more than 3,000 per day. In 2009, it was more than 13,000 per day. And in 2012 you can bet it will be many more than that.

Just think about the number of messages you get just going to work. How many cars or trucks with affixed ads pass by? How many billboards do you see? How many stores with special signs do you pass? How many commercial messages pour out of the podcast or radio you're listening to? How many ads in the browser blink at you as you sit down at your desk?

But there's an interesting counterbalance to this that is just starting to emerge. The growth of Web-based social networks is starting to filter that advertising for us. The social graph is becoming one of many "filters" that we as consumers are consciously and subconsciously deploying to deal with the onslaught of information. Our brains tell us that there is a correlation between content that comes from our network, and its quality. So, as marketers we've learned that context and relevance are more important than ever.

But wait — this is short term. When ALL marketers catch on — the pendulum will swing back and the noise will become just as loud. So, ultimately, while we will technically be able to deliver more and more relevant advertising messages to our consumers — ultimately the filters will become tighter and tighter and more and more expensive to get through. **Thus, the only way we can maintain long-term success is to continually engage people.**

Bob Knorpp, the host of BeanCast Marketing Podcast and president of The Cool Beans Group, explained this well in a July 2011 article on AdAge.com. He said:

> *"When we set out to create digital stories, maybe it's time we left out models completely. Instead of looking for ways to get eyeballs on our videos or clicks to our pages, maybe we need more focus on creating multilayered experiences that keep people involved, immersed, and interacting. And maybe the measurement of effectiveness should not be based solely on page views or 'likes' but on distributed participation of fans both online and offline ... [This] challenges the notion that engagement ends with a click, a comment, or a share ... Maybe it's time we looked at the Web as something different."*

This is really the ultimate argument for content marketing as a strategy — and hopefully it can become an important part of your case for innovation and content marketing.

In 2012 and beyond, it's the relationship that matters. We have to not only GRAB attention, we have to HOLD attention.

Why Must We Be Engaging?

In 2009, Gallup released the results of a study titled "Customer Engagement as a Core Strategy." They came up with a series of 11 questions — which they called the CE11 — that measured customer engagement. The results were astonishing. They found that organizations with "fully engaged" customers had a 23% premium in terms of revenue, profitability, and the relationship with that customer. Conversely, they found that "disengaged customers" provided a 13% discount against those same metrics. Put simply, a fully engaged customer is much more likely to buy from us, continue buying from us, and actually promote our product or service to their friends.

How do we learn this art of engagement?

Well, let's first continue to consider the practical. As you assemble a content marketing strategy focused on creating engagement with real people — a very specific audience — you do so within a very specific context. Call them pre-requisites if you will, but there are three things that are most likely true in your situation:

1.   You are already being asked to do MORE with LESS — and in much shorter time frames.

2.   Good content marketing practices tell you to "become a media company (or publisher)" within your industry. You will need to enlist more internal resources than just marketing to produce all this content. The "who" you need to engage may be a much wider audience than just the usual prospective customers. In short, you may need to engage customers, or dissatisfied customers, or others with your content marketing.

3.   You need to somehow measure engagement and your results.

Let's look at each of these.

You Have to Do More with Less.

All marketers certainly have felt the pinch over the last few years. Budgets have been down, headcount has been down, and resources have been stripped. Yet the need to produce more and better results has never been more pronounced.

If you've won the business case for content marketing and your organization is like most, you're pulling money from other, more traditional marketing tactics (e.g., TV, radio, and print) to pay for content marketing. You're shifting dollars, rather than getting more. At the same time, your need to offer more and deeper solutions to your customers is growing — which inherently means you have to produce more content, from more people — and with more care.

You Have to Become a Media Company.

Today, it's simply not enough to be noisier, cheaper, or more efficient — you have to become a content production house, covering the industry in which you operate. You need experts to show your customers how to use your products or services. You may even have to be entertaining. This is really the idea of "content marketing" and how we're all becoming media companies.

Becoming a media company requires that you engage both internal and external resources; however, you must do it in a way that doesn't end up being more expensive than it already is. Therefore, you have to track your progress.

You Have to Find Ways to Measure and Report Your Progress.

To remain relevant to your audience, you have to be interesting. And because you have to do more with less, you have to do it in a way that doesn't feel like the same, tired old marketing. New methods will require that you invent new ways to report progress and measurement against your goals. It will be meaningless to deliver a 40-page series of analytics reports to your CEO and expect her (or anyone else for that matter) to derive any meaning from it.

In value-selling methodology, there's a great lesson that says that C-level executives care about one simple thing: increasing revenue. Everything else — costs, margin, talent, etc. — falls from that one metric. If you can convince them that you can increase revenue, you can sell them.

That's an important lesson for us as content marketers. With the buckets of information at our fingertips, it's not a dashboard full of numbers that will win the day. It's a few.

That's not to say that we shouldn't measure a great many things. In fact, we should be measuring everything we can. But if we use the 33,876 granular analytics measurements we're tracking to try and justify our budget to our CEO and CFO, we've lost the game before we've even started playing.

WHO are Your Customers?

With these three prerequisites — this context — in mind, how do we prioritize our content marketing strategy to help us succeed? How do we move partially (if not holistically) to a content-driven process that helps us engage our constituencies more effectively on the Web, in person, and even in print?

Well, quite simply, it all starts with WHO. And remember — it takes more than one WHO to make an impression. As traditional marketers, we typically lean forward and skip right to figuring out WHO our target personas are. But let's also remember that in addition to knowing WHO we are talking to, we need to know who WE are. As Lao Tzu said: "He who knows others is learned; he who knows himself is wise."

At its best, a content marketing strategy involves exercising a different creative muscle than many of us may be accustomed to. What content marketing is not — and certainly is not for the scope of this book — is a way to discuss your identity as an organization. We're not here to re-design your identity or business strategy. Content marketing is not trying to figure out a unique "position" to differentiate from competitors. We are not trying to figure out "tag lines" and "brand statements."

Rather, content marketing is here as an expression and a magnification of what you already know. At its core, we use content marketing to find OUR story. We are strategizing a conversation that WE want to have that engages OUR audience and one that will keep them (and us) engaged over time. At its best, this story is unique to us. For example — Southwest Airlines understands its unique story. They sell one of the most commoditized services around — plane rides. But what they are really providing — and what their story really is about — is "democratizing travel" so that everyone can fly.

However, while the "who" that is YOU is incredibly important, we're not going to spend time helping to explore it. There are plenty of other books and consultants who can help you if you have that challenge. We've built this content marketing strategy process over many successful engagements with clients small and large — and have seen it work. But in the end, this process will be a generalized approach to a unique process: yours.

While throughout this book we suggest timelines and levels of effort and even maps you can follow — you will find that they work best when coupled with your unique creativity and individuality. Therefore, this means that the process that follows (and frankly everything in this book) will be unique to you and your organization. So you have to know and understand who YOU are first.

In short, as you go through this book and others on content marketing, consider them a well-worn trail. You'll almost assuredly find new shortcuts, and even new wonders along the way. And, because this is our effort to engage a conversation — we hope you'll share your success stories as well.

Demographics Don't Work Anymore

Do you really know WHO your customers are? The first thing you need to understand is that personas are NOT demographics. Demographics are simply attributes of a population (e.g., age, gender, race). Marketers have used demographics for years as the way to target market segments. If you take nothing else away from this book, take this: Stop using demographics as a means of targeting your consumers.

In fact, just recently, television network CBS and its Chief Research Officer David Poltrack teamed with Nielsen to suggest that it is time to replace demographics with a new model for TV planning and buying. They conducted a study across 20 different categories, including health, beauty, household, pets, and food, and confirmed some earlier studies on demographics. As Poltrack said, "There is no link, none, between the age of the specified demographic delivery of the campaign and the sales generated by that campaign."

If demographics don't work any more, what next? We have to start thinking of our buyers as people — alive and different and separated by their behaviors — rather than their demographics. Of course, these people will represent "segments" (or groups) of our consumers — but they are nonetheless individuals that we can identify and service. Let's take a look at how we can better understand them.

Step 1: Develop Your Personas

There are entire books and lengthy papers online about how to develop buyer personas. They discuss conducting complex segmentation studies, setting up focus groups, and other very detailed ways of getting to "know" your consumers.

We believe that while you can — and perhaps should — go through a comprehensive buyer persona and content mapping and segmentation exercise, many times this just isn't feasible. We understand that in the real world of marketing, getting things done in a purely academic way just isn't realistic, given the real-time pressure for results and your existing resources.

However, figuring out WHO you are talking to is vitally important — and walking through a buyer persona development exercise is important. You're going to need one persona for every distinct group to whom you are marketing. In other words, if the person goes through a different buying cycle, they're a different persona. Is that different for a man or a woman? Well, if you're selling jewelry the answer is most definitely "yes." But if you're selling enterprise software, the answer is probably "no."

For example, let's say you're in charge of marketing for a technology company and your Widget Integration Management Program (WIMP) solution is marketed to IT directors and CFOs at financial service companies. You would have two WIMP buyer personas: the IT director and the CFO. Each persona has different engagement cycles that ultimately lead them to a purchase decision.

What do you need to know about these people? The easiest way to think about this is by asking the following questions:

1. **Who is he or she?** Here we want enough detail that we can describe our persona like we would a good friend.

2. **What's their need?** This is not "why they need our product" (although we should know that too). Rather, what needs for content/information do they have that we can tie back to the IDEA of the story we want to tell?

3. **Why does he or she care about us?** This is why our persona wants to engage with us. What can we uniquely provide to him or her?

4. **What unique value proposition (UVP) do we offer this persona?** We should know (although we may not use it heavily) how our product or solution will uniquely help this person meet their needs. We will want to imbue our content marketing strategy with this UVP — and use it to direct our overall story.

So let's go back to our WIMP solution.

In order to properly understand our personas, we need to know what drives them. What does their day look like? Again, you can see how you might spend days and months determining a level of detail around this. And, again, our recommendation is that you spend enough time so that you have the ability to describe them like you would a relatively good friend.

How do you get there? Start by interviewing customers or prospective customers. Certainly your sales and customer service people have met or spoken with customers. Get their input, too.

In our example, let's say that we've talked to several people and now have enough information to create a persona for our IT director. Here's what it might look like:

JEREMY — Our IT Director

Jeremy is young (mid 30s) and he works at a bank. He comes in every day and supports the organization's networks and he's the typical geeky IT guy. He responds well to email, but he's not really a phone guy. He's frustrated because he can't tie all the office computers together and see their status on one dashboard. His company is growing so quickly that he seems to continually be chasing his tail, behind in fixing the computers around the office. It's affecting his home life and making him rather unpleasant to be around. Jeremy would love to be able to see problems with a computer before it crashes. In theory, this is where your WIMP solution comes in.

What's Jeremy's need? It's not just the product. See, Jeremy is so busy and so focused and so junior that he doesn't even know where to start solving this problem.

He's not a business guy and would have no idea how to build a business case for this. And while he's seen the Web site for the WIMP solution — and is vaguely aware of the product — he doesn't really know much about the details of how it gets implemented in the enterprise.

Why would Jeremy care about us? Well, we can help him feel better. The WIMP story doesn't involve telling Jeremy that he's inefficient, and it's about more than creating a more efficient IT environment. The

WIMP story helps Jeremy feel GREAT about what he can do. At WIMPY, we are about creating IT heroes. We want Jeremy to have a "secret sauce" that gives him a superpower.

But, ultimately, our unique selling proposition (USP) to Jeremy is that our WIMP solution will uniquely enable him to save more than 10 hours per week in saved calls, repair time, and waiting for replacement parts. That means we can make Jeremy look like a rock star (his personal win) to his colleagues while we enable him to be 25% more effective at his job. So the question now is what kind of content do we need to create and get in front of Jeremy in order to 1) give him confidence, 2) convince him to take the time to build his business case, and 3) evangelize it in his organization so that a budget will be created for our product?

That's building a persona.

Let's get emotionally attached to our personas by giving them names and making them real. And then, let's add some context, which leads us to our second step.

Step 2: Create the Engagement Cycle

Just as in real life when you meet someone, determining what you want to say to a persona is a combination of two things: content (which is a function of your point of view) and context (you have to determine the correct time and place to start the right conversation).

The traditional way of advertising is to take our point of view and just climb up on top of our virtual stage and start talking. The theory goes that if we blast loud enough, long enough, and in the general direction of our personas, that eventually we'll reach some of them. Is it any wonder that we have historically looked at 2% as a "best-practice" conversion rate against our advertising?

Things are different now. The buying process has changed. The consumer now controls the engagement with you — and it's up to you to have a relevant conversation with them from the very first time you meet.

But the reality is just as we can't be prepared to have EVERY conversation about our product or service at any time — we won't (at least initially) have the resources to prepare a well thought out content piece for every piece of the consumer's buying cycle for our particular product or service.

Additionally, our customer's buying process can be chaotic and non-linear. This is why, historically, we've developed our sales process (or funnel) so that we might put some order to this chaos and have common language in our business for the categories of sales opportunities. Depending on our business, we may categorize our consumers as "visitors" or "leads" or "prospects" or "readers" and (of course) "customers" or "members."

Even if we don't have a formal sales process, to some degree, we intuitively do try to deliver against one. Most organizations, to some degree, try to deliver a relevant message to the customer while they're in the sales process. For example, if you're selling widgets online, you always try to cross-sell and upsell AFTER the user has put items into their shopping cart. If you're selling big ticket items, your salespeople probably have a well-defined funnel that leads pass through (lead, prospect, qualified, etc.) and they give out case studies and testimonials after they've become "qualified."

But today we're trying not only to create a "customer," but to create engaged subscribers. And, while it's important for us internally to map our conversation to our sales process, we must remember that whether it's our shopping cart experience, a traditional lead nurturing sales funnel, or converting customers into evangelists, that this sales process is an internal and artificial process that we place on top of the buyer.

Our buyer doesn't care one bit about our sales process. Our sales funnel does not capture the emotional and realistic decision points that the buyer goes through during his or her "buying process." And in fact, our goal may NOT be to have the "customer" purchase anything at all. It may rather be to have him or her "refer a new customer" or "share their story."

To deliver our best content at the right time, we need a better, more granular process. We need to combine our internal sales process with our customer's "buying" process and develop something new ... something we call the engagement cycle.

An engagement cycle is a defined process that our audiences go through as we help them increasingly engage with our brand. We use it to map content to both sales and a consumer engagement process to help deliver the right conversation at the right time.

Let's look at each of the processes separately before we layer them together.

Map Your Personas to Your Sales Process

Our sales process is how we watch the consumer proceed through our sales and marketing efforts. Our funnel might be very well organized — as in the case of enterprise B2B marketing or considered purchases in B2C sales (e.g., a car or house). In these cases, there will be very defined and tight conversion layers where each stage is defined by the consumer behavior (lead, prospect, qualified, etc.).

However, if we run an eCommerce or brick and mortar shop, we might have looser or more generalized sales processes. It might just be visitor, browser, shopper, buyer — and these stages happen within seconds. Or, if we're a publisher, the funnel might be visitor to subscriber. Regardless of the time or our name for it, the sales cycle is how we identify those customers who:

- Know nothing about us
- Then know something about us
- Then are interested in what we have to offer
- Then compare us to other solutions
- Then do what we want them to do.

Going back to our WIMPY solution for our target personas, we have a fairly simple sales funnel process. We have:

- Contacts — people we've contacted or have some level of introduction with

- Leads — people we've identified who have an active interest in our solution

- Qualified opportunities — leads we've qualified as having interest and a budget, and a purchase of some kind is imminent
- Finalists — qualified opportunities who have reduced us onto a short list of one or two options and we are competing with
- Verbal/contract — where we are the chosen solution and we are in the negotiation process.

Your sales funnel may be more — or less — complex than that, or completely different. But regardless — there's some level of stage; there's some kind of funnel.

Now, let's start to build our content segmentation grid. You'll do this along two axes. The first axis is the personas, and the second is your sales funnel.

Once you have your grid, start filling in the cells with your existing or new content items. We'll discuss how to develop your story and your content in Chapter 3 — but you no doubt have existing content, so your grid might ultimately start to look something like this: (See chart on next page.)

Content Segmentation Grid

SALES	CONTACT	LEADS	QUALIFIED	FINALIST	VERBAL
Jeremy, IT Director	White Paper 1 White Paper 2	Our Blog	ROI Calculator	Case Study 1 Case Study 2 Case Study 3	
Cheryl, CFO	White Paper 3	Interview w/ CEO	Webinar / ROI Calculator		

PERSONAS

One thing you may notice in this example is that if we've created a bit of content marketing most of it is focused at the top of the funnel. This is almost universally common, so don't worry if this is true for you as well. We almost always start a content marketing strategy by focusing on awareness and education, which is almost inevitably at the top of the funnel.

One benefit of this exercise is that it very often points out that your content marketing is either very light or very heavy on one stage or one persona.

Once you are armed with your content segmentation grid, you are ready to take the next step, which is to layer in each persona's buying process.

Map Your Personas to Their Buying Cycle

David Meerman Scott, the best-selling author and marketer, has a wonderful bit of stagecraft with which he often opens up his talks. He asks how many of the people in the room think their consumers care about their product. As a few hands go up, he corrects them and says "no — no one cares about your product or service. All your buyers care about are themselves." He goes on to advise how you can develop a much more conversational tone with a minimum of buzz words and discover how you might help your customers. These customers will then, in turn, naturally gravitate to what you have to offer.

This tactic, to any traditional student of marketing, should come as no surprise — as it's exactly in line with the famous quote from Peter Drucker:

"The aim of marketing is to know and understand the customer so well, the product or service fits him and sells itself."

But didn't we say at the beginning of this book — and aren't we hearing everywhere — that marketing has fundamentally changed?

Yes. It has. But that change is not just that "digital" commands such a significant piece of the media buy. No, the true fundamental change is the buying process that the digital technology has enabled. In other words, the Internet hasn't been a fundamental change for us as marketers — it's been a fundamental shift in the way people BUY.

Let's turn our attention toward the buying process — which is almost always more complex than the sales funnel. This is how your customers buy from you, or once they've bought, what you want them to do next. What's their process? For your product or service it might vary by product — or by persona — but what you want to do is map out how your customers buy from you. Let's go back to our WIMP Widget Company once again as an example. The customer's buying cycle looks like this:

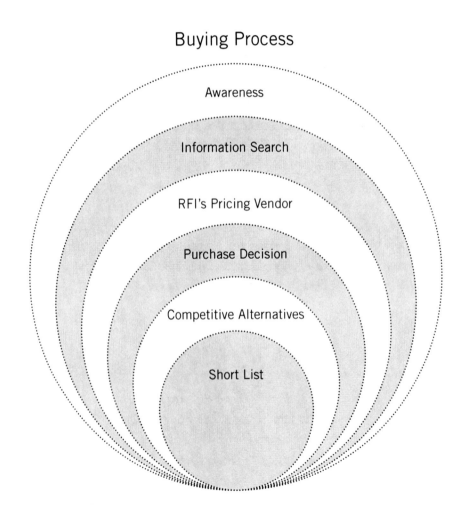

Buying Process

Awareness

Information Search

RFI's Pricing Vendor

Purchase Decision

Competitive Alternatives

Short List

We've represented the buying cycle here as an orbit — because it's not necessarily linear. In fact, during the buying process, consumers often jump in and out of orbits as they move closer in. But as the consumer does move closer to the center of gravity, the focus on what they want becomes more pronounced and what they're looking at becomes more limited as they go through each phase. So, for example with the WIMP solution, each phase looks as follows:

- **Awareness/education** — the consumer is trying to figure out what options exist.

- **Information search/vendor selection** — now they're searching for information and finding solutions for their problems; this may be the first time you get a phone call.

- **RFIs pricing/vendor information** — you've been identified — so what makes you better? What is your pricing for this solution?

- **Purchase decision** — which is not always the last step. Many times people will go through researching a solution to their needs, and then decide to NOT make a purchase. But those who do decide to make a purchase will go BACK to vendors and do a final comparison.

- **Competitive/alternative searching** — the Google searches begin. Ever gotten a call from a consumer that feels like they're late in their process? This is where they are. This is the feature comparison stage. In many cases, the consumer may be surprised by what's missing (or what's there) and may go all the way back out to awareness/education.

- **Short list** — where the solutions are looked at very closely and then a contract for the sale is presented.

Armed with this knowledge, you can develop a buying process for your personas and against each product. And we're sure you've realized by now that the number of buying cycles can be high — especially if you have a number of products, or personas (or both).

You also, no doubt, can see that in some cases there may be a "buying" process where there is no existing sales process. For example, when you have customers that you're targeting for a "renewal," or where you want customers to share their story. The alignment of these processes may be very different where you are driving consumers to an initial "purchase decision" vs. one where you are driving them to an upsell or even just an evangelistic conversion. It will be up to you to know when and where to create separate processes for your content, and where there may be overlap.

But the key is that when these two processes are laid together, you end up with a nicely defined engagement cycle — one that takes into account both the customer's "buying" intentions and your internal sales process.

Step 3: Create the Customer/Content Segmentation Grid

So what does our engagement cycle look like, mapped in with our content? (See chart on next page.)

As you can see, we've mapped in the sales funnel with contacts turning into leads, and then being qualified, and going to finalist (or short list). But then, under that, we've mapped the buying process, awareness/education, and so forth.

You'll notice there's overlap with the sales funnel and the buying process. There are actually many more conversion layers — or decision points — through the buying process than in our sales funnel. But this gives us a way to start to get a common vocabulary and a common way to map out our content marketing strategy.

We may find, for example, that we have a lot of content developed for leads that are in the "Awareness/Education" stage, but we don't have a lot of content for leads that are in the "Information Search" stage. This tells us that we may want to spend some additional time developing content that not only educates our audience to the benefits of our *type* of solution, but also positions our company as a provider of it.

As we mentioned in the beginning, it's not a requirement to go to this extent. And you certainly don't have to develop content segmentation grids for every product, or every process. Maybe you should only do it for the process to which your new content marketing initiative is directed. Or maybe you only need to do it for helping to move customers to evangelists.

Content Segmentation With Buying Cycle Highlighted

SALES	CONTACT	LEADS		QUALIFIED		FINALIST	VERBAL
BUYING CYCLE	Awareness & Education	Information Search Vendor	RFI Vendor Information	Make the Purchase Decision	Alternative Searches	Short List of Vendors	Contract
Jeremy, IT Director	White Paper 1 White Paper 2	Our Blog		ROI Calculator	Webinar	Case Study 1 Case Study 2 Case Study 3	
Cheryl, CFO	White Paper 3		Interview w/ CEO		ROI Calculator		

PERSONAS

Or maybe you should map all but one product to just the sales funnel. That's valuable. Or you could map just the buying cycle — that's the second best. In the end, creating an engagement cycle and mapping that with your personas to create a complete content segmentation grid can be a powerful way to see where there are gaps in your story.

So let's just quickly review ...

1. We developed our personas — and defined the WHO we wanted to deliver our content to. We developed enough specificity that we can become emotionally attached to them. We gave them names, and made them real.

2. We built up our sales process — either from what we knew or what we gathered from the processes we use to move people through our marketing and sales process. We documented this funnel and identified all the stages for the various funnel conversions, from first awareness and contact, to opportunity to sale. And we identified that this can be applied to any marketing and sales process.

3. We looked at the buying process — and we understand that it's non-linear. It's a chaotic orbit that our customers follow when trying to make a decision about a level of engagement with our brand. It may be an initial sale, an upsell, a renewal for another term, or something as simple as sharing their story in an evangelistic way. In any case, just as there is content to support the sales process, we need content to support the buying process.

3. We created an engagement cycle — by combining the sales and buying processes and mapping them together. Our engagement cycle is a designed process that helps us to deliver the most relevant content to the most relevant persona at the most relevant time.

4. We mapped this to create our customer/content segmentation grid — and we can see that our content can be much more highly targeted when we align it an engagement cycle.

As content marketers, our most important goal should be to ensure that our stories are aligned with how our consumers research and come to realize that they need our product or service. To that end, it's about constantly seeking those ideal moments, or decision points, when we can make those connections. It's like when you're in a conversation with someone, and by the look in their eye, you realize that you've just said the exact right thing at the right time.

The more of those "moments" we can create, the more likely we are to succeed with our content — and our marketing. And the more closely we understand our customers and the various journeys they take along their buying process, the better chance we have of creating those moments.

Speaking of journeys — it's time to move ours on. Because now that we understand who we're talking to and the moments we can create — cue the dramatic music.

It's time to tell our story.

Chapter 3
Create the Journey:
Developing Your Pillars of Content

*"There are only two or three human stories,
and they go on repeating themselves as fiercely
as if they had never happened before."*

—Willa Cather

*"Pleased to meet you, hope you guess my name.
But what's puzzling you is the nature of my game."*

—The Rolling Stones

I f there's one question about content marketing that gets asked almost as much as "what's the business case," it's quite simply: what do we talk about?" And that's what this chapter is about — developing your story.

If you remember only one thing from this book — make it this:

Good content marketing is alive. It is your story. It is conscious. It is about emotion.

Way back in 1960, Theodore Levitt's classic paper "Marketing Myopia" appeared in the *Harvard Business Review* when he was still a lecturer in business administration at Harvard.

Even if you're not familiar with Professor Levitt, or his article specifically, you'll no doubt know of its classic theme of asking yourself "what business are you in?" This is the often quoted and rarely acknowledged cautionary tale of the railroads not realizing they were in the "transportation" business, rather than the "railroad" business. Levitt wrote brilliantly on how to succeed in marketing by thinking of customers' needs, rather than selling product. Yes, even in 1960 the main themes of content marketing already existed.

But one of the other examples that Levitt used in that paper — and the one that most often goes forgotten when talking about the subject — was his pointed critique of the Hollywood studios. In 1960, the "movie" business was being threatened by a new-fangled technology called television.

If you think Hollywood is running scared with digital content in 2012, you should look back to what happened in the 60s. 1963 was the worst year for U.S. movie production in 50 years. The major studios only made 120 releases that year (as a point of reference, there were about 560 films released in 2010). It was during the 60s that the major movie studios, which had been owned and operated by individuals, were taken over by many of the multi-national companies that we associate them with today. As TV invaded the consumer's home and changed their relationship with content, the "golden age" of movies in Hollywood changed, arguably, much more substantially than is happening today.

But, also much like today, while Hollywood knows how to tell a great story, they didn't really deal with technological progress very well. Levitt chastised the movie business and in that seminal paper he said:

"Today, TV is a bigger business than the old narrowly defined movie business ever was. Had Hollywood been customer-oriented (providing entertainment) rather than product-oriented (making movies), would it have gone through the fiscal purgatory that it did?"

Replace the word "TV" above with "Web" or "social media" and we'll see that there's still much to learn from Professor Levitt.

This is the point: The idea of content marketing and creating engaging content isn't new. It challenges everything we know, because of the fundamental changes. But it really changes little that we actually do. The Web has finally arrived. It provides the unprecedented insight we desire as business managers while we communicate with our customers, employees, and partners much more seamlessly than ever before. In the end, though, we still have to be effective storytellers.

In 2012 and beyond, the main reason we will be successful in our respective businesses is because we have a specialized expertise — and we can create a differentiated experience for our customers with that expertise. We (ideally) have a passion for the BIG idea that this expertise represents. We provide a differentiated product or service — and we've asked ourselves the question "what business are we really in?" Assuming we still agree with that answer, developing the content in our content marketing strategy is developing the stories of us. It's the big ideas that we represent. It's the differentiated experiences we want to create. It's what we REALLY do for a living. For better or worse — it's that simple.

Think about it this way: Take a look at your local air-conditioning company. On the surface, you may think that the story of the air-conditioning technician is to fix or repair the air-conditioning system when needed. But actually, the air-conditioning company's story should be centered around the idea of a home comfort expert for that specific region. Think about that … an expert in home comfort. What the air-conditioning technician really does for a living is provide home comfort solutions to homeowners in his or her area. Once that story is arrived at, the content ideas can begin.

We Are All Storytellers

In his book *A Whole New Mind: Why Right-Brainers Will Rule the Future,* Daniel H. Pink talks about the emergence of storytelling as an enormously important aspect of how we will become successful. He discusses how the age of the "knowledge worker," the person who manipulates data, is changing. With the progression of information technology and globalization, he makes the point that "high concept" aptitudes will form the new age. He defines "high concept" as involving …

"…the capacity to detect patterns and opportunities, to create artistic and emotional beauty, to craft a satisfying narrative, and to combine seemingly unrelated ideas into something new. High touch involves the ability to empathize with others, to understand the subtleties of human interaction, to find joy in one's self and to elicit it in others, and to stretch beyond the quotidian in pursuit of purpose and meaning."

In short, what he's saying is we're all storytellers. And in content marketing, your stories are your "pillars of content." They are the

WHAT of what you are going to say to your personas.

How do you go about developing these stories? There are no hard and fast rules, but you can certainly apply the same techniques and structure used for novels, short stories, and movies to your content marketing.

This is not to say you should force a structure onto the story you want to tell for your business. As we know inherently from great novels and movies, sometimes a wonderful story breaks all the rules — and comes at us from left field. And, certainly a comedy is structured differently than a drama or a thriller.

But, we can go back and look at classic storytelling and structure as a helpful map to guide our way. We can look at the characters in our story, and use the classic "hero's journey" from Joseph Campbell to give shape to the story we want to tell.

Now at first this might sound a little corny, and a bit too esoteric for a business book. But remember: the point of developing our story is that we are trying to differentiate from our competition. Look at the word. Differentiate means telling a DIFFERENT STORY — not the same story told incrementally better.

As you're well aware, sequels are almost always highly unsatisfying. So too, if we tell the same story as our competitor but with a slightly better punch line, we simply create sequels. So stay with us here, and let's walk through developing your pillars of content.

The Stages of a Hero's Journey

In his book *The Hero with a Thousand Faces*, Campbell outlined what he calls the "monomyth" — which is a pattern that many believe can be found in almost every narrative around the world. It can certainly be seen in classic Hollywood storytelling. Campbell's point is that story-telling across time all shares a fundamental structure and can be summarized into this journey.

In 1992, screenwriter and story consultant Christopher Vogler took Campbell's structure, modernized it for today's audiences, and reduced it down to 12 stages in his book *The Writer's Journey: Mythic Structure for Storytellers & Screenwriters.* This made the stages much more approachable for today's writers — and is now mandatory reading for any novel or screen writer.

One of the main points that Vogler made was that by aligning a story with classic structure you can quickly determine what is "missing."

Vogler's hero's journey is this:

The Hero's Journey

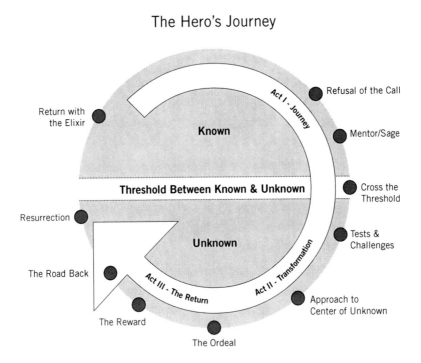

1. The Ordinary World.

This is the hero's world as our story begins — or in reality just prior to the beginning (sometimes told in flashback). This is where we learn about our hero and his nature. We learn his capabilities and his outlook on life. He is flawed and we are anchored to him. In many cases, he or she may make a wish to be lifted from this ordinary world (think Dorothy just before the storm) — or others may wish it for them.

2. The Call to Adventure.

Very soon into the beginning of the story, our hero will receive a call to action. It may be a threat to his (or his loved one's) safety, or the ordinary world in which he lives. This doesn't always mean it's a violent threat. It could simply be something that threatens to disturb our hero's ordinary world in some way. The key is that it invites a quest. Think about the scene in *Casablanca* when Ilsa asks Sam to play "As Time Goes By" in Rick's casino.

3. The Refusal of the Call.

This is a very important part of our story. Even though our hero may want to jump eagerly into the challenge, there will be something to overcome. It may be fears or deep personal doubts, or it may be a reluctance to leave the ordinary world because of the fear of leaving something behind. This is what helps us identify with him as one of us. It's the same fear we have. You've seen this scene in a million different crime thrillers. The cop starts to walk out of the lieutenant's office. "I'm retired" they say — just as they're about to be lured back into the biggest, most challenging case of their life.

4. The Mentor or Sage.

Then there is a timely visit from our hero's mentor or sage. This mentor will provide guidance and teaching and insight. He may provide practical training — or simply words of encouragement. It is ultimately what propels our hero to begin his or her quest. Think of the classic scene in Star Wars (episode 4) when Obi Wan Kenobi makes his first appearance and tells Luke of his innate skills and family history.

5. Crossing the Threshold Into the Unknown.

As the hero prepares for the quest, there is a threshold between his ordinary world and the world he must enter in his quest. At this point, he may have second thoughts again, or he may go willingly, but as the threshold presents itself it is a significant change — and typically means there's no going back. Harry Potter *literally* does this in the first book when he passes through the magical wall at the railway station to Platform 9 3/4. It's clear his life will never be the same.

6. Tests, Challenges, Friends, and Enemies.

Now in the realm of the unknown, our hero is confronted with ever more challenging tests. They are physical, mental, emotional — and these obstacles are thrown across his path to thwart his success. Along the way, he will meet people who can be trusted — and some who can't (other types of challenges). The hero's skills are tested to the limit here, and every challenge gives us much deeper understanding into his character — and helps us feel like we are sharing his experience. In the *Pursuit of Happyness*, Will Smith's character goes from down on his luck at the beginning of the movie, to evicted, homeless, and living in a shelter before finally coming back.

7. Approach to the Center of the Unknown.

As our hero conquers challenges, we are building toward his approach to the largest, most demanding challenge. It may be a physical place, or emotional — but it is something that the hero has never conquered before. But before the hero can enter the center of the unknown and face the ordeal, special preparations must be made. You've seen this in countless movies and novels — where the characters all must regroup, plan, and/or prepare for the big set piece of the story.

8. The Ordeal.

Whether a physical test, or deep emotional crisis, the hero must face the final ordeal in order to survive in the unknown. The hero must draw upon all the skills he has, plus all of the ones (including friends') that he has gathered upon the journey in order to overcome this challenge. This is not the climax, but rather when we finally see our hero transformed in action. Think of the movie *E. T. the Extra-Terrestrial*, when Elliot's new best friend (E.T.) appears to die on the operating table.

9. The Reward.

Once the challenge has been overcome, the hero is rewarded with the transformation into the new "state of being." She emerges from the ordeal different than when she entered the unknown — and often it is with a prize. It may be a job, a crown, money, love, greater knowledge, or even reconciliation with an estranged loved one from the ordinary world. But whatever the prize, it tees up the last piece of the journey. Think of Dorothy "winning" the broomstick that she was challenged with stealing.

10. The Road Back.

This is the reverse of the call to action — where our hero had to cross into the unknown. Now our hero must (or wants to) return home with his reward. Now, as he prepares to return, the ordinary world, he is changed and is seen in a new way. He might be vindicated, grown up, or now a king; but he is different. Think of *Indiana Jones and the Last Crusade*. Toward the end of the movie, Indiana has successfully obtained the Holy Grail, and learned the lesson of his father — and pours it over his father's wound and saves him. He now realizes that it's not about the reward — it's about going home.

11. Resurrection.

This is the climax. The hero must have his confrontation with something representing "death." It's now about something far greater than the hero's existence. The outcome will also affect his ordinary world and those he has left behind. If he fails this challenge he will not only fail, but will have failed everyone. He must overcome the worst situation possible. Think of *Rocky* — in round 14 he is literally knocked down and out. His "ordinary world" of Adrian actually closes her eyes — she can't watch. He manages to get up and make it until the final round, where he is clearly on the verge of taking Apollo Creed out when the final bell rings. He has gone the distance.

12. Return With the Elixir.

Finally, after the resurrection stage, our hero returns back to the ordinary world a changed hero. He or she is a new person, having learned many things and having acquired new skills and friends. Her return may bring fresh hope, and/or help to those in the ordinary world. But in the end, it's really a new perspective for everyone in the ordinary world to consider. Almost every romantic comedy employs this with the "magic speech." Our changed hero runs through the rain, avoids oncoming cars, and jumps through some cataclysmic hoops to reach his love just before she leaves "forever." He gives her the "magic speech" of how he's changed, and how together they will be stronger and better than ever. And, at the end of the speech, we know he's changed. He's back in the ordinary world — and gets the girl.

Now – The 10-Step Brand Journey

In this section, we'll examine how you can use the hero's journey to develop your own pillars of content — your own stories. We've reduced Vogler's stages down to 10 steps for developing your content marketing brand journey.

But before we jump in, know that this is just a framework, not a "to-do" list or a template. The structure is meant to provide a platform for you to develop a way to TELL the story or maybe to discover what's missing from your existing story. It's not a TEMPLATE for the story. That's an important distinction, because your story will be unique to you, your brand, and the experience you are trying to create.

Feel free to add to, customize, delete from, and/or otherwise modify this framework. Use it as a tool to help you develop your pillars in a way that lets you differentiate your content marketing from your competitors.

The content marketing brand hero's journey. (See chart on next page.)

The CM Brand Hero's Journey

One approach is to use this process as a tool for brainstorming. You can also use it to create a story map to plan out your editorial calendar and channels strategy. Or maybe you just want to use it as a checklist to see where your story fits along a pattern. Whatever you do, remember that you are looking at this framework as a CREATOR of the story — not as a participant in it. And after a while, you'll see that as you continue to create content, this structure will become an inherent part of your thinking.

So here goes:

Step 1: The Conventional Market.

This is your brand's world — and as you brainstorm your pillars of content, you should know and be able to define the conventional. What does your market look like? Where are your competitors situated? What is the reality for your customers? Why do they currently identify with your brand?

Step 2: The Challenge.

This is your big "what if?" What if XYZ were actually true? What would the world look like if you could actually realize that Big Hairy Audacious Goal (BHAG) that you've set out for your brand? What is the call to adventure for your product? What's the big promise?

Step 3: Rejection of the Challenge.

Why hasn't this been done? Why haven't *you* done it yet? What's the pain that the conventional market feels now? What will you need to add to your story to let your audience know what will be left behind? Are you conflicted about this? What will be the effect of this change on your existing brand?

Step 4: Appointment of the Sage.

Who in your company (or outside of it) can help you take this adventure? Who will provide guidance for your brand as it makes this journey? Is it you? Is it your CEO? Or, do you even have that person? Is it more than one person? Can you get someone external for this? Will you need to conjure an imaginary character to act as your sage or mentor? Who can stand in front of the world and credibly tell your audience that you are going on this journey together?

Step 5: Crossing Into the Unfamiliar.

This is where you burn the ships so that you can't go back. Ultimately, in your content marketing, your brand must take a definitive point of view that is differentiated — and it will cross into your new "what if" idea. This is the unknown — and you are exploring. How will you communicate this crossing into this new idea — this new adventure? And how will you lead your audience into this new unknown with you?

Step 6: Map the Road of Challenges.

Part of this step is unknown to you as an author, but you can use it to determine how you'll gather friends. Or maybe you'll take a strong point of view that may actually create enemies, or controversy. Who will your brand align with? How can they help you move forward? What tests to your brand's legitimacy will it face in the unknown? Who will be the naysayers? What tests and challenges can you plan for?

What skills will your brand need to address?

Step 7: The Final Challenge.

As your brand faces these challenges, attracts and aligns with friends, and establishes a differentiated point of view, it should establish itself as differentiated — as a leader. What will it ultimately achieve? What learned skills (or attributes) will your organization take into the final challenge? What will that final challenge be?

This is the culmination of your story. In the larger sense, you may never want your brand's (your hero's) story to end. And this content marketing campaign may be but one episode in your story. But this final challenge is what you have to OVERCOME to get to the possibility of the "what if" …

Step 8: Looking Back.

Take a look back at the ordinary world. Your brand is different now. How do you show that differentiation?

Step 9: The Final Renewal.

What ambush could — or will — your brand face now that it is different? What will the competition say about you now — and HOW do you continue on? Your brand's story is never going to end and you are ready to continue on your journey — but there may be huge challenges now that you are different. How will you overcome them?

Step 10: The Celebration.

This is you realizing the dream. Celebrating. The final part of your story.

There you have it — the structure. It can be used across one small content marketing initiative — or across an entire strategy of content marketing across the enterprise. Changing the level of hero from product, to brand, to service can make it more interesting, and enables you to explore ever-more creative "webs" of stories between them.

This story structure — which is inherently linear — can also help you structure your content into a story map. The story map helps to organize your pieces of content across a timeline. It compels you to think of your content pieces as "chapters" or "scenes," and can help reveal the gaps. It may resemble a high-level editorial calendar – but is structured with a focus on telling your complete story.

To summarize, you use persona and *engagement cycle maps* to ensure that you are nurturing content along the non-linear path of getting people to "engage" with the story; you use *story maps* to ensure that you're building story structure in a linear way that tells a complete story from beginning to end.

Can your audience be placed in the middle of your story? Maybe. That's for you to decide as the creator of the content marketing.

If you're a little lost at this point, that's okay. After all, you haven't put this into practice yet. Let's take a look at an example to see how this actually works in real life.

REAL LIFE EXAMPLE — Case Study
PTC — Developing a Content Marketing Strategy for a New Product

In the late 1990s and into the 2000s, computer-aided design (CAD) software was going through a chaotic feature war. Companies were being acquired, the market was consolidating, and the software was becoming more and more bloated with features. PTC was the undisputed market leader — but there was really no innovation happening in the marketplace. The feature bloat, along with acquired technology and legacy software, meant that CAD software was big, unwieldy, and very hard to use. One historian noted that the "kind of innovation that drove the industry forward in the 70s and 80s [seemed] to have died."

PTC services more than 25,000 customers in the industrial, high tech, aerospace, defense, automotive, consumer, and medical device industries. And, in 2010, they had an idea that would shake the CAD software market.

The company wanted to introduce Creo, a new kind of suite of CAD software. The differentiation was quite technical, but really centered on four breakthrough ideas: Deliver better usability, complete interoperability, the freedom from technology lock-in, and better functional innovations. Through this new product, PTC would reinvigorate and redefine the design market and its position in the marketplace.

Building the Story for PTC

We were brought in to help build a content marketing strategy for PTC's new product launch, which they wanted to develop a new blog and social Web strategy around. Here is how we used the brand story journey as our platform for creating the pillars of content.

(Note: you can find the complete case study at www.contentmarketinginstitute.com).

Step 1: The Conventional Market.

We first defined the world that PTC found itself in. It was painful — and people knew it. Their target personas were frustrated by the state of CAD software. No one really enjoyed using it anymore — and in fact, training was a nightmare. The conventional world of CAD software was one that was stagnant, and filled with pained and unhappy users. No direct competitor (in fact, no one) was addressing this — and everyone tended to try and talk around it.

Step 2: The Challenge.

PTC's VP of Marketing Rob Gremley asked the big "what if?" in our first meeting. He asked, "What if we could completely re-define what product design software is?" He went on to say that "25 years ago, PTC re-defined CAD software with innovation. And now, PTC will do it again."

In short, the call to the challenge was that PTC wasn't just introducing a new product — they were introducing a new vision for what design software should be. We used this as the central part of our challenge.

Step 3: The Rejection of the Challenge.

But then we asked ourselves, "why hasn't this been done?" And, more importantly, "why didn't PTC do it sooner?" And we also asked whether the audience would "believe" — or would they be cynical about this? What would happen if PTC did this and failed? How would we address that in our story?

We decided that the brand hero of this story (PTC and its new product) would have to address this head on. We would intentionally create an admission of "guilt." PTC knew that it had been part of the problem. Our character was flawed — but had realized that a change bigger than itself was necessary.

Step 4: Appointment of the Sage.

It was clear early on that we would need several mentors and sages. We would have different audiences here based on our persona development — and we would need both technical and business sages to author content. We chose the main "authors" and built them into our story as the ones who would "carry the torch." We needed PTC's own product design managers, as well as influential bloggers and writers, to be on our side — to help us on our brand journey. Additionally, we would make sure that PTC — since it was designing a product that would "redefine designing products" — would "show its work" and be more transparent with its "friends."

Step 5: Crossing Into the Unfamiliar.

Crossing into the unfamiliar would happen after the launch. We talked about the challenges that introducing a new product and vision for software would create. We discussed, at length, the risk of people holding off on new software purchases until the new software was launched (what would happen to existing sales). We pondered what would happen if we started to tell this story and then the software failed to meet expectations. We knew that once we started down a journey and began to build a community there would be no going back.

So we built the pain into the story structure. The first three months would be all about the frustration. This would get the audience on our side. It would help us and our hero identify with them. Then, once we had them — we would give them the vision. We would start telling the story from a visionary point of view — and phase out the pain.

And to address the unfamiliar, we would make sure that the story said that any existing purchases would be "new-product ready." In other words — we would protect the audience to take this journey with us.

Step 6: Map the Road of Challenges.

We planned long and deep about the challenges we would face. We discussed the naysayers and how we would respond. We talked about the competition — and our position on that. We discussed the pitfalls we could see by splitting the story up across months. We mapped these into the timeline and developed story points around each one.

Step 7: The Final Challenge.

To meet the goals and to continue to build legitimacy, we knew PTC would need friends along the way. As we switched from pain into visionary, we reached out to influential friends (other bloggers) and shared our point of view. Again, the PTC goal was not to "own" this process, but rather to "lead" this new vision. This meant they would need to include other points of view as well. We also knew that the final challenge would come upon the software launch date. We planned to phase in our friends/bloggers and include them heavily in all storytelling and in the final event itself.

Step 8: Looking Back.

Once the product was launched, we created a storyline and structure for the content to follow. This content "claimed victory" and showed how PTC is now exhibiting all the great characteristics of an innovative software company ... that PTC is, once again, "setting the standard."

Step 9: The Final Renewal.

For PTC the Final Renewal represented the product itself and sales. What would the initial rollout look like? We had to develop a story around what would happen post-launch. What would the story be after the launch of the new product? We had to make sure that we weren't ambushed by the complacency of "product launch," and then stop. PTC would need to continue driving thought leadership through the blog.

Step 10: The Celebration.

For PTC this was the product launch — and knowing that their story would continue on.

Culmination of the Structure

After taking this structure — and using it as a brainstorming and content creation platform — we then transformed our ideas into three pillars of content that would make up PTC's new Web site/blog:

A. Customer-focused Content — this content became known as the "reinventing design" content. It was named after our brand's "call to action." In our story structure, it would start with a *laser focus purely on the end-user*. It would be used to set the stage for how PTC had focused on the "frustrations" of how design software could be better. It would focus on the pain and frustration of the product design process. We would build the excitement of a new way — but acknowledge the past failure of anyone to take action. Then, as we moved through our story — it would start to change. It would talk about "best practices." It would feature guest posts by the friends we would begin to align with — the industry leaders. It would feature links to external content that discuss thought leadership in the space. The theme of this content would align as the go-to-market strategy evolved — starting with frustration, and then widening out to provide more best practices as the product and vision gained awareness — and ultimately would show success as the "vision" of Creo was realized.

B. PTC-focused Content — this content was called the "behind the scenes" content. It would be carefully and thoughtfully published — and yet would be high velocity enough to maintain interest. We knew that as our story progressed there would be challenges and tests. We knew that people would be skeptical. And we recognized the irony that the company was "designing a new product" that would change "product design." Therefore, we would focus this part of our storytelling on how the company would "walk the walk" of the new vision. We would take the veil off and address the tests and challenges that would come up along the way. This is where we let our sages and mentors have their voice — to help our brand overcome these challenges.

C. PTC and Customer-partnered Content — this content was initially nicknamed "in search of Creo" and was later called "reactions." It was really designed for the latter part of our story, but would play an important role in the early going as well. This content would be created early on to show PTC's commitment to the "vision" — not just the product. And then later — once the product was available — it would be part of the "final renewal." This is where we would share success stories of people who were using the new product and embracing the brand.

Next we took these three pillars of content and structured the story across a "three act structure" of a story map to come up with a high level thematic editorial calendar.

Story Map

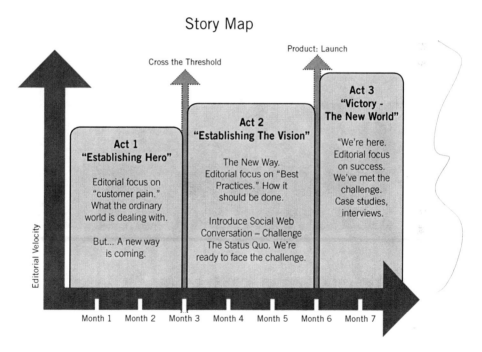

Developing a story map.

We looked at the first act of "establishing our hero" as the first month of content. These posts would be really focused on the customer and their pains. The second act would establish the vision and address our challenges. We would increase velocity here and focus in on the design process of PTC, as well as the curated community content. Then, finally, as we led up to the product launch date, we would lean BACK into the visionary piece and really establish PTC as the thought leader for this new paradigm.

We also applied our content to the engagement cycle (for this campaign) and started to map out where each persona would enter the story. This was important because it helped to inform how much "backstory" would need to be introduced to each piece.

Engagement Cycle To Story Map

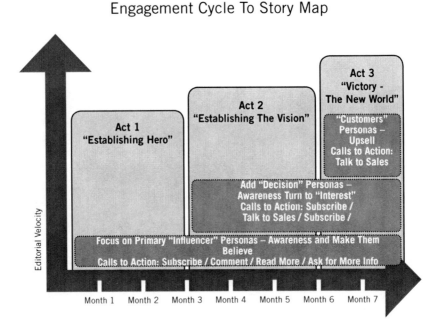

Mapping the engagement cycle to the story map.

For example, we knew that potential consumers who were coming into the story in the "second act" might not have seen the "feel the pain." They would only be getting the "vision." Certainly there's nothing wrong with that. But it gave us an idea to make sure to include information about that first phase of content in each piece of content that came next. We would link back to "pain points" or other elements mentioned in the first phase, as a way to give the audience access to the beginning of the story if they needed it.

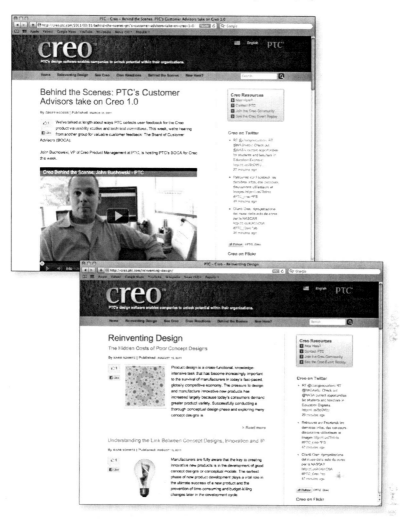

Now, of course, this story is still being told — but if you'd like to read the entire case study, you can find it at the Content Marketing Institute Web site.

One of the questions you may have at this point about the PTC story is "why a blog" and "why posts" as opposed to a white paper program, a print magazine, or through Twitter or Webinars. Which brings us to our next chapter: Once you've created your story, you have to determine what channels you'll use to distribute it. It's time to write out your content marketing plan.

Chapter 4
Digging Your Channels

"In Russia we only had two channels. Channel One was propaganda. Channel Two consisted of a KGB officer telling you: Turn back at once to Channel One."

—Yakov Smirnoff

L et us introduce you to Minnie Maud Hanff — one of the first practitioners of content marketing. Minnie was a freelance writer and jingle composer in the early 1900s. In late 1902, the advertising manager for Force Food Company asked her to come up with a campaign for their new wheat flaked cereal.

The typical American breakfast at that time consisted of fried eggs, meats, and potatoes. It was the meal that started the "farmer's day." But as more Americans started to work in offices at the turn of the century, the call for lighter, faster breakfasts started to become the order of the day. Successful products like Cream of Wheat had begun to make their way onto consumers' breakfast tables. But, basically, in today's market equivalent, Minnie had the challenge of creating a campaign for health food.

Minnie and artist Dorothy Ficken decided to go a different route than the traditional, straightforward advertising that carried the day. Instead, they created a complete story featuring a character named Jimmy Dumps. Jimmy was a fat, small, morose man — but when he ate the cereal he was suddenly transformed into Sunny Jim.

The two women produced funny little jingles, poems, and comic images that told the story of Sunny Jim. These "stories" appeared in magazines, on billboards, and on the sides of trolley cars starting in the spring of 1902 and going into the fall. By the time 1903 rolled around, Sunny Jim went the early 1900s version of "viral." Consumers by the thousands started producing their own "jingles" and stories about

Sunny Jim and sent them to the Force Food Company. Sunny Jim's image appeared on the sides of hundreds of buildings. A popular magazine, *Printer's Ink*, stated at the time about Sunny Jim that "no current novel or play is so universally popular. He is as well-known as President Roosevelt or J. Pierpont Morgan."

And success? Well, in 1901 Force Cereal was produced in one single plant in Buffalo, New York. Three years later, more than 360,000 packages of cereal were being produced per day in three production plants across the country.

What was the secret of Sunny Jim? First, Minnie and Dorothy told a funny, compelling, and ultimately shareable story about something bigger than just cereal. It was a story about being transformed by eating. And, really importantly, they told the story in the right context — through magazines, trolley cars, and images on billboards.

Context in a Digital Strategy

Frankly, "distribution" is where most content marketing and social media plans begin. **And it's why most fail.** So, if you started reading this book at this chapter — stop right now and go back and read the other ones first.

We've watched it happen. The CEO or VP or owner of the business slaps the airline article that provocatively suggests *"Your Business On Facebook"* on your desk and asks "where are we on a Facebook strategy?" Social media consultants crop up everywhere proclaiming to have the answer to a Foursquare strategy, or a Twitter strategy, or a LinkedIn strategy.

And, to be fair, remember that from 1994 to 2008 (or so), just having a digital channel strategy was okay. Everyone accessed digital content using a "computer-like device." It might have been a desktop computer or a laptop computer — but in reality we could look at it just like we did television. Regardless of whether our content was delivered as an email or a Web site, our digital strategy was simply a broadcast of content to a computer that was consumed by an audience. Everybody knew what this "digital strategy" looked like. Is it any wonder that we applied all our broadcast media measurement strategies to it? We looked at reach, frequency, impressions, pageviews, and ultimately conversions to measure our effectiveness.

But today — and moving forward — it's different. It's become doubly as complex as we've seen an exponential increase in both the interfaces in which our content appears — as well as on what kind of device experience (e.g., mobile, tablet, computer, television, etc.). Context in our digital strategy is hugely important for two reasons:

- Digital content is now a conversation — a two-way street
- The types of interface that consumers use to interact with our content has exploded.

Now, as marketers, and specifically paid media buyers, we've of course been aware of context and messaging — because we've thought about it as we put together our advertising strategies. It's because we spent money to place that messaging, that we thought long and hard about optimizing the context for that placement. And we used ratings points, share, demographics, impressions, pass-alongs (for print), and even conversion rates as a measurement of just how right or wrong our contextual assumptions were.

And when we were right — when we delivered the right advertising to the right person at just the right time — that was when our media planners earned their gold stars. Context is the magic bullet. It's actually the one thing that closed the deal.

But here's the challenge. We've rarely, if ever, taken the same care into how we strategize our digital content. Historically, for our Web site "digital channel strategy," we've thrown all the content that "prints to fit" up on our Web site in hopes that we'll somehow get the "long tail search." Maybe we looked at usability, or other elements of a more holistic content strategy, and wondered about our "target audiences" and the "users" of our Web site.

For example, up until this year, we were geniuses if we had a "mobile compatible" version of our Web site. If our main Web site didn't just completely break down in the iPhone browser — or whatever mobile device our CEO has — then we were good to go.

Obviously that's not enough anymore. The average household now has two desktop computers, three laptops, two video-capable cameras, a digital camera, two cell phones, a scanner, three TVs, eight remote controls, three DVRs, some type of gaming device (e.g., a PlayStation® or Xbox), and at least one Kindle, iPad, or other tablet device. The availability of content has simply become contextual. Audiences now EXPECT content when, how, and where they want it.

So far in this book we've showed you how to identify your personas, develop your pillars of content (the stories you want to tell), and segment your content into both your personas' buying cycles and your internal sales cycles. Now it's time to choose how you are going to "place" that content. What channels are you going to use to distribute your content? To answer this question, you have to consider the CONTEXT in which your audience will view the content, and then use that to alter the content accordingly.

At this point, you need to go back to your buyer personas and add in a contextual layer to your strategy, sales, and engagement cycles — this will help you optimize the delivery of your content marketing for contextual placement. Start by asking:

- What language should we produce this content in?
- In what device context will this content be consumed (device, interface, channel)?
- Why will people want this content through this channel?
- What do we hope they will do with this content?

You need to develop a plan that takes all these factors into account. Let's walk through the steps of creating that plan.

Creating Your Channel Plan

There are seven basic considerations for developing a content marketing channel plan:

1. Situational analysis
2. Channel objectives
3. Content/conversation plan (how you're telling your story)
4. Metrics
5. Personas addressed

6. Content management process
7. Editorial calendar

Let's look at each of these:

1. Situational analysis.

This is your first step and the universal one that addresses all the channels. This is where you use the information from your persona and engagement cycle mapping to look at your current "situation" to determine where you can have the most impact with your story.

Obviously some of your existing marketing efforts (e.g., your blog and Web site) will come into play here. The idea is to map what you currently have, to what you need to effectively tell your story. Ask yourself:

1. What do we **already have** that helps us tell this story (e.g., an existing Web site, blog, Facebook page, Twitter account)?

2. What **must change** in order for us to tell this story (e.g., do we need to add a blog, develop a separate blog, create or revisit our social Web strategy)?

3. What **must stop** (if anything) for us to tell this story (e.g., do we need to stop using Facebook and divert our energy to a blog)?

Out of this situational analysis will come some prioritization, budget consideration, and more tactical things that need to get done.

2. Channel objectives.

This is where you map objectives of the channel to the engagement cycle (remember these are tightly woven with your ultimate goals). And it's perfectly okay if a channel only "contributes" to another channel.

For example, based on the goals of your content marketing, and the story you are telling, you may decide that the primary objective of your Facebook page is to create increased and loyal traffic to your ultimate content (let's say it's a blog). In order to drive that traffic, you may need to create a following on Facebook. So your first "objective" for the Facebook page will be to "build your likes" to create that community.

3. Content/conversation plan.

This is how you map the channel to the larger story structure. This will usually take the form of an outline or narrative and is used to organize your content plan for the channel.

For example, in the situation described above — because your primary objective for the Facebook page is to increase loyal traffic to your blog, you want to build a community. So the first part of your content plan for Facebook might be a "contest" or some other type of community-building action to build your "likes." The second part of the plan might kick in once you've reached some "goal" (e.g., conversions, number of likes, etc.); then you'll begin refocusing your content to drive specific personas to your blog. You can use your imagination to see how this might be multi-layered as you continue your community building and refocusing of content.

You need to consider context here as well.

For example, let's say you're talking about a "mobile channel" and your channel objective is to build subscribers to your blog or Web site. And let's say you post lots of really valuable, long-form content on that blog. Maybe an initial content plan for that "mobile channel" would be to produce a different, shorter, or more mobile-specific category to that channel, knowing that your mobile persona only has time and bandwidth for a very short version of content that they may want to read later. Here, you are fulfilling the "contextual need" of your mobile persona.

The "conversation" aspect of the plan applies if the channel is meant for conversation and not just content consumption. We discuss the "process of content marketing" in the second half of the book, but as part of your content plan here, you need to account for the "challenges" and "friends" that you may acquire in any channel, and plan to engage accordingly.

4. Metrics.

We use the word metrics here very specifically, as opposed to key performance indicators (KPIs) or "results." With as many channels as you already have working, against all the different campaigns — and as your content marketing will inevitably overlap into your channels — metrics are what you want to track here.

KPIs will play an important role in your content marketing — and we will discuss them at length in Chapter 11. But here, metrics are "goals" that will align with your story. For example, you might say "with this contest we're running on Facebook, our goal is to get 1,000 'likes' over the next two months before we move into the second phase of our story."

5. Personas addressed.

Looking back at your persona mapping, certainly not every channel will address every persona. So for each channel you are considering, you should identify which personas will be addressed.

Once you are done with your channel plan, look at it holistically and make any adjustments. You may find that you have done a great job of creating a channel plan that fails to address your most critical persona. Whoops. Or, you may find that you're trying to address too many personas through one particular channel – and it makes better sense to split them. For example, Dell has multiple Twitter accounts used for customer service, discounts, and general information.

6. Content management process.

We will look at content marketing processes in the second half of the book; for this exercise, you just need to ensure that you have a method and process (e.g., people and tools) to manage the content and conversation for this particular channel. What will you manage? Who will do it — and how?

7. Editorial calendar.

Lastly, you'll need an editorial plan for the channel. This will map to your global editorial calendar — but doesn't identify dates or times yet. The purpose of the editorial plan is to define velocity, tone, desired action, and structure for the content for this channel.

For example, for your Facebook page you might have the following:

Velocity — three posts per day

Tone — friendly, funny, and with a tongue-in-cheek attitude
Desired action — we want them to click through to the blog
Structure — 10 to 20-word post, plus pictures (if applicable) and
"conversion link."

So there you have it — the seven basics of a content marketing channel
plan. As we mentioned earlier, just keep in mind that you can create
multiple channels. You're allowed to have more than one blog, or
multiple Facebook pages – and you don't have to launch them at the
same time. For example, you may find that two different types of
Facebook pages are more appropriate than just one. Or you may find
that you want to later add a Twitter account specifically for a subse-
quent "chapter" of your content marketing story. There is no one right
way to do things, so experiment, get feedback, and continue to evolve
your channel plan.

The content strategy defines the channel strategy — not the other way
around.

**The Content Marketing
Institute** recently released its
"Content Marketing Playbook"
covering 42 different content
marketing channels to choose
from — from blogs to info-
graphics — with a case study
for each channel. The playbook
is free and is available at
http://bit.ly/cmplaybook.

What Form Does this Channel Plan Take?

Well, it depends — but one of the easiest ways to organize your plan is to assemble it in a spreadsheet or some kind of grid where you can see things across a number of matrices and fill in the gaps accordingly.

A simple channel plan. (See chart on next page.)

A good content marketing channel plan frees you from the constraints of any one content channel. As your blog efforts wane, or as social media channels come and go — or as your success on any one of them ebbs and wanes — you won't be trapped into a singular channel. No longer do you have a "Twitter strategy" — but rather a content strategy that utilizes micro-blogging. So maybe Tumblr will be a better and more effective channel for that. Pop it in and try it.

In the end, a good channel plan will ultimately lead you to specific strategies for each part of the story you are trying to tell.

A Very Simple Channel Plan

CHANNEL	NAME	STRUCTURE	TONE	DESIRED ACTION
	Main Corporate Site	News Section - 250-Word Blurbs announcing new items	Professional	Click to blog (all phases)
	Product Micro Site (New Blog)	Blog with 500-750 word posts	Casual/conversational	Subscribe Phase 1 - Add "White paper download Phase 2"
Blog	Main Corporate Blog	Cross Linking - Making sure existing posts are linking into new Micro site	N/A	Link to blog posts
	Sales Twitter Channel @Sales	Conversational	Friendly - Focused on being our "broadcast" platform and online conversation. Add to existing Twitter content.	Click through to blog posts. RT's of our information.
	CRM Twitter Channel @CRM	N/A	N/A	N/A
	Linked In	New Linked In Group	Asking questions to generate conversation	Follow and join group on Linked In - Click through to blog

Chapter 5
Putting It All Together

"If you can't describe what you are doing as a process, you don't know what you're doing."

—W. Edwards Deming

"In order to succeed, we must first believe that we can."

—Michael Korda

Whew! How are you doing? Is it too much to take in? Does it seem overly complex? Trust us — it's not. These are tools and practices that you as a creative marketing person already have innate talent with.

Remember, at the beginning we said that a successful content marketing program focuses on the process of creating and managing content. The purpose is to tell your story so that it attracts and retains customers. You just create — or curate — valuable, compelling, and relevant content in order to maintain or change a behavior in your customers.

You are simply becoming storytellers. The first half of this book is simply figuring out WHO you want to tell your story to, WHAT story you want to tell, and WHERE you want to tell it.

The second half of this book shows you HOW to manage the strategy you've created. We'll get into the process of content marketing and how to know if you've been successful. But before we get into the HOW, we have to make sure we're clear on the WHAT.

And, beyond all the things that we talk about in this book, the most important thing you can do to ensure that your content marketing will be successful is *BELIEVE that you can be successful.*

Lessons from Linus

Do you remember the story of Linus — alone in the pumpkin patch?

It's a cold night and Linus is eagerly awaiting the arrival of the Great Pumpkin. As the rest of the Peanuts gang ridicules him, Linus holds fast. He KNOWS in his heart of hearts that the Great Pumpkin will come and leave presents for him and the rest of the children who are "sincere." Sally sees him alone, and as little cartoon hearts circle around her, she joins him in the pumpkin patch — sacrificing her trick-or-treating with the other kids.

"I'm so glad you came back," Linus says. *"Each year, the Great Pumpkin rises out of the pumpkin patch that he thinks is the most sincere. He's gotta pick this one. He's got to. I don't see how a pumpkin patch can be more sincere than this one. You can look around and there's not a sign of hypocrisy. Nothing but sincerity as far as the eye can see."*

And that's the lesson for us as content marketers. We are about to "make public" a strategy for our brand's story. Beyond anything, we have to believe in it. We have to be authentic, and as we make the ever-important transition from theory and what we believe (our strategy) to practice (how we will manage it), we must fight like hell to prevent our efforts from getting watered down.

Yes, there will be a great tendency for your content marketing to be watered down. As you develop your story, the kids in the pumpkin patch will gather around and throw every doubt they can into your belief. What will start as quiet hallway conversations a few weeks into your process, can become full-blown conference room debates:

- "We can't talk about competitors here."
- "What's our official position on that — we need to add that into every post."
- "We've never talked about that before — we have to delete that."
- "We don't compete well on that issue."
- "Aren't we helping our competition with that post?"
- "We need a lot more persuasive content on this blog ... what's the ROI?"

And your strategy may change. Maybe you'll omit one of the more "controversial pillars" in order to add some "persuasive content." You might be tempted to put in a traditional call to action for a "free trial" or "discount" on every page. Guess what will happen?

The Great Pumpkin of Success will pass you by.

If you follow content marketing best practices, learn from past successes, join the conversation, and stay true to the sincerity of your story, you *will* generate results.

Take a lesson from Linus and bring out your passion and your willingness to be wrong. Remember — even though content marketing has been around for more than 100 years, the *practice* of content marketing is still relatively new. As you develop your content marketing strategy, there will be those who come into your patch and just don't understand. They may ridicule you — or tell you that they just "don't get it." Like Linus, you may find that you initially attract some of your colleagues into it, only to watch them lose their nerve and give up just before you have to commit.

But believing is a powerful tool. And making sure your content marketing stays true to your conviction is the key ingredient necessary to make sure success doesn't pass you by …

What Will Your Strategy Look Like?

So let's get practical. Once you've completed your content marketing strategy — what does it look like? So far, you've:

1. Built your business case
2. Developed and mapped your personas
3. Structured the journey of your story
4. Defined your content marketing channel plan

How do these actually translate into deliverables? And what do these deliverables look like?

Well, how much and in what format you actually need to document your strategy will certainly be unique to your business. For small and limited content marketing initiatives, we've seen success from just walking through the process and not documenting much at all. In other, larger organizations or initiatives, documenting everything and adding mapping or even separate executive summaries can make sense.

The key is (as you've probably noticed) that these areas are not completely linear in nature. There are bits of each process that will inform and change other bits. For example, if you change your story substantially, you may reprioritize personas — which may affect your channel strategy and even your overall goals.

You have to synthesize ALL the information you've gathered into a cohesive strategy that fits what you're trying to accomplish. To that end, in general, you can look at four specific documents to help you codify this process:

1. The Content Marketing Strategy Document
We like to create a Word version of this document, along with a PowerPoint. This document contains the business case (to the extent it needs to be documented), the high level "results" of the persona development and mapping, the story map, and the high level of the content marketing channel plan.

2. The Persona Development and Mapping Document
This usually comes in the form of a document — although it may contain pictures as well — and provides the more detailed mapping and descriptions of the various personas that will be targeted, as well as the initial content mapping to the engagement cycle (the combination of both the sales process and the buying process).

3. The Content Marketing Channel Plan
This is the more detailed plan for the individual content channels; it can usually be best formatted in a spreadsheet.

4. The Global Editorial Calendar
The global editorial calendar is an aggregation of your channel plan and actually looks at content production as well as the editorial schedule. It can take many forms, although its final realization will be tied closely to your process (which we will cover in the second half of the book).

5. The Resource Plan (Occasionally)

This is a common document when your content marketing strategy is performed as a brand new initiative. After you've defined your strategy, completed your persona development, identified your story and mapped your channels, you'll find there are a large number of tasks to be completed. You'll need to assign resources for these tasks – and in many cases, it may affect your timeline or budget. To download a sample of a full content marketing strategy starter document, go to www.managingcontentmarketing.com.

And with that, we're about to add more tools to help us move forward. We're stepping into Part 2 —The Process of Content Marketing.

PART TWO
THE PROCESS OF
CONTENT MARKETING

Chapter 6
The Four Stages of a
Content Marketing Process

"If you don't create change, change will create you."

—Unknown

"I don't believe in the no-win scenario."

—Captain James T. Kirk

Congratulations.

You've created a strong business case and a strategy for your content marketing initiative. You've created a set of deliverables that provide you with a great baseline of information. And, while many of the components of this strategy may feel familiar to you and to your team, much of what follows now will feel like a brand new concept in your business. And guess what? It is. It's going to change everything you know, and really nothing you actually do.

At its very core, content marketing is something you as a marketer have been doing since day one. You provide valuable information that supports your product or service without a "hard sell." Content marketing is about celebrating what makes your business unique. It is, inherently, about making the business more social and more human. It's about telling the story of the unique YOU. It's about what YOU and YOUR ORGANIZATION stand for. It's about the ideas that YOU bring to the table. And, just like there isn't one way to have a great conversation, nor one "correct" way to tell a story, your content marketing strategy will be unique to you. And that's how it changes everything you know.

The process of content marketing — of telling your story — is new to you. Learning how to transform your organization into one that creates "subscribers" may be different than what you or your team has known in the past. And that's the critical piece. Now that you have a strategy in place, you have to make it real.

So here you are — you're passionate. You believe in your cause. But you have this new strategy that no one in your business has ever executed. You have a business case and a game plan for creating stories that have yet to be written, and conversations yet to be had. How the heck are you ever going to create and apply a generalized, repeatable, and measurable process over the top of that? Where's your template? Help! Where's the map?

At this point, there are probably several things racing through your head:

- What happens if we fail to get return on all this content that we're producing?
- What happens if no one cares what we're saying?
- What happens if our customers start saying negative things about us when we put ourselves out there?
- How are we going to get all the internal stakeholders involved in this new strategy?
- Why will anyone in our business care?

Is there even a way to *win* this game?

In the Star Trek universe, there is a training exercise designed to test how a Starfleet cadet will react to a no-win scenario. The test involves a simulation where a civilian vessel called the Kobayashi Maru has been crippled. Life support is low and all aboard will surely die if the captain doesn't rescue them quickly. The problem is that the ship has the unfortunate circumstance of being crippled on the wrong side of the Klingon neutral zone. That's bad news. In short, it's a test that no one has ever faced before — and one that no one can win. It's a test purposely built to test the limits of a leader's skills as he has to facilitate a losing process.

But, of course, our hero James T. Kirk doesn't believe in the "no-win scenario." In Star Trek II: The Wrath of Khan — and subsequently revisited in the J.J. Abrams movie Star Trek — Kirk is the only cadet to ever beat the Kobayashi Maru test. How? He cheated. Or, in his words, he "changed the conditions of the test."

That's a great lesson to keep in mind as you start this journey to create a brand new process to facilitate your shiny new content marketing strategy. This new process operates at a speed, agility, and nuance that most organizations just simply aren't used to — and in many cases simply can't keep up with. Remember, we're not only defining and creating a "publishing" process — we're also inventing a "listening" process (aka, setting up listening posts). And we're opening this process up to a much wider, coordinated effort between all of the stakeholders in the organization. This means that we'll be engaging everybody from marketing, sales, customer service, product development, finance, legal — and even the C-suite. The old adage is true — now everybody *really* does have two jobs: theirs and marketing.

Example 1: P&G Allowed the Story to be Written Without Them

In the early part of 2010, Procter & Gamble introduced a new version of their highly successful Pampers product. According to an Ad Age article at the time, P&G executives were hailing this new product as the "iPod of baby care." The product was a redesigned diaper that while 20% thinner than the previous diaper, was much more absorbent.

The challenge came when P&G introduced the product to a "test market." Instead of repackaging the new product, they decided to put the new diapers in the old packaging. And, unfortunately, the company didn't communicate this change at all. Word started to spread online that this new product wasn't as good as the old product, and groups started to form online asking the company to "bring back" the old product. Pretty soon, there were multiple groups — including a Facebook group, and groups on "mommy blogs" that were all loudly protesting the new product.

The lesson here is that P&G let the story start without them. One of the best answers to the question of *"what happens if we do?"* is *"what happens if we don't?"* In many cases, you have the option to tell your story — or your story can tell you. In this example, P&G didn't realize that their "subscribers," in the absence of a story, would just go ahead and start to make up the story themselves.

P&G simply fell back on their more traditional product marketing thinking. The company had anticipated some "backlash" from new consumers until they could ramp up their marketing programs, and had factored that into their launch plans. In fact, in that same *Ad Age* article, Jodi Allen, VP of North American baby care at P&G, was quoted as saying *"All the data we have to date, in particular from our consumer 1-800 line, is that the complaints are well within what we were expecting and considerably lower than we've seen with some of our previous innovations."*

But remember — the world has changed. Even five or six years ago, that small number of complaints in a test-market would have gone largely unnoticed, and would have been a risk that a brand like P&G could safely take. But today, that risk is a bit like lighting a small firecracker in the middle of an oil field. Sure, it might just go pop. But it also might light your whole world on fire.

In a retrospective analysis of the campaign, many marketing and social Web experts commented on how the P&G team could have used content and social media channels to announce the change and respond to consumers. And given P&G's size, you can certainly argue that despite the amount of chatter, this "mistake" didn't derail the product launch — at least to any degree that P&G couldn't spend some of the $9 billion that they receive in annual Pamper's sales on fixing it. But the simple and most profound lesson is that it was an uncoordinated process. A successful content marketing process should have or (maybe more importantly) could have supported the launch. So whether you call it a "mistake" or a "missed opportunity," either way a successful content marketing process could have made the launch better.

Example 2: JetBlue Rewrites Their Story

On Aug. 10th, 2010, JetBlue Flight 1052 from Pittsburgh to New York's JFK International airport taxied into the arrival gate. What happened next is the subject of some speculation but, after an argument of some kind, flight attendant Steven Slater had a "take this job and shove it" moment.

Slater stood up at the microphone as the plane was on the tarmac, proceeded to tell the woman he was arguing with exactly what he thought of her (filled with expletives), grabbed a beer from the plane's galley, then slid down the emergency evacuation chute. By that evening, Slater had been arrested and released on a $2,500 bond. By the next morning he was a folk hero.

JetBlue's Facebook page lit up over the following hours, filled with a range of comments. Some of them were screaming that Slater should keep his job. Others were saying that all JetBlue flight attendants were horrible. Suddenly, almost everyone had something negative to say. And, what did JetBlue say in the hours following the incident? Nothing.

Is this the Kobayashi Maru? Despite all our best efforts to create a story, are we just destined to have the world start without us — and leave our brand heroes abused, confused, or misused in the wake? Are we, as marketers, just going to have to live with the fact that sometimes the conversation will escape our ability to lead it, and that our content marketing platforms will become a free-form hate fest?

Enter Captain Kirk.

The process that JetBlue had in place, by most accounts, really turned what could have been a horrible story into (arguably) a great opportunity for branding. In the hours after the incident, JetBlue's silence had many wondering if the company was being muzzled by its lawyers. And many also posed the question whether there was any way to stem the tide of the groups forming online.

But then, on the afternoon of Aug. 11th, JetBlue posted a relatively tongue-in-cheek blog post titled, "Sometimes the Weird News Is About Us." [http://bit.ly/jetblue-weird] It was short and to the point.

They explained why they couldn't talk about the incident (because there was an investigation and they respected the privacy of the employee). They also linked to a funny clip from the movie Office Space, acknowledging that sometimes we all want to bust up a few fax machines. But they also pointed out that JetBlue employed 2,300 other passionate, caring employees. These people were still on the job, cared about passengers, and would continue to operate in the JetBlue way. In short, whether JetBlue realized it or not, they inherently changed the rules of the test. They rewrote the story that was being told.

What happened over the next few days was really interesting to watch. The sentiment seemed to turn bit by bit. Over the next few days, hundreds of comments appeared on the blog post. JetBlue occasionally chimed in, but only to correct a factual error or keep things from being inflamed. It was the cinematic equivalent of the action hero keeping everyone calm as the guns blaze overhead.

Pretty soon, bloggers and the press took notice. Peter Kafka at AllThingsD blogged about JetBlue's "comeback." A post at MarketingVox said that JetBlue "seemed to survive" the crisis. Then, over the next week, Jetblue's Facebook page — with the occasional reminder that people could go to the blog to post comments — seemed to go back to normal very quickly.

How did JetBlue's process work so well? How did they rewrite the conditions of what seemed like an unwinnable test? The overarching success factor was, no doubt, a well-honed process. A few key things stand out:

1. **They waited for the RIGHT amount of time to pass.** Not too fast, and not too long. No knee-jerk reactions — but no "corporate silence" either. Unlike previous mistakes with other companies, where the company jumps and reacts too fast before all the facts are known, JetBlue waited. Maybe this was the lawyers — but it took guts for that marketing team to not say ANYTHING.

2. **They made JetBlue the HERO and re-introduced the ordinary market.** With one post, Steven Slater was no longer the hero of the story — JetBlue was the hero. They didn't write "sometimes we

have a flight attendant go bad" or "sometimes an employee goes nuts." No, they wrote "sometimes the weird news is about US."

3. They gave the HERO a renewed call to action. JetBlue made it clear that they understood the frustration and felt the public's pain. But they wanted the public to realize that they still had 2,300 employees tackling the challenge of getting people to their destinations. They were moving forward.

4. They told just the RIGHT STORY to their personas. They didn't speak in lawyer-talk or immediately go to the whole "TSA, FAA compliance and concern for security blah blah" thing. They also didn't shift the blame or make Slater out to be a martyr. But neither did they roll over on their back and throw all the employees under a bus. They balanced the popular sentiment with the reality that "yeah, sometimes work is tough — but we've got 2,300 other employees who are awesome and are ready and eager to serve you."

5. They employed their strategic channel strategy and MOVED the conversation to a more appropriate place. They immediately asked everyone to continue the conversation at the JetBlue blog.

Ironically, Steven Slater ultimately failed at telling his own emerging content marketing story. After a few news outlets began to report that he may have made up the whole story about a rogue passenger, the negative conversation started to appear on his own Facebook page. And new groups started to form, including a Facebook page called "Steve Slater is a Liar."

This reinforces the point that JetBlue was wise to wait a bit — but not too long — before commenting. These stories usually have some kind of twist, and JetBlue positioned itself to take the story whichever way it turned.

Now it's Your Turn to Play the Game

Whether you are managing the content marketing process for a B2B product company, a non-profit, a government agency, an online retailer, a media publisher, or your own small consultancy, the process you put in place will have broad implications on your strategy.

The Content Marketing Process

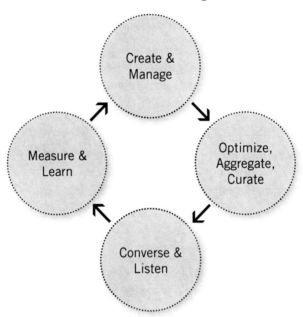

How do you create an optimized process that will support your content marketing and set you up for success? You need a framework of a human-driven process (facilitated by technology) to close the loop on managing an online and offline content marketing engine. This framework of a content marketing process has four stages:

1. Create and Manage
2. Optimize, Aggregate, and Curate
3. Converse and Listen
4. Measure and Learn

Let's take a look at each.

1. Create and Manage.

The key to a compelling story is compelling content. To create that content, you're going to need to assemble a team, develop a workflow that makes sense, establish the rules you'll all play by, and agree to follow them. We'll look at this more closely in Chapter 7, Welcome to Workflow. In Chapter 8, The Tools of Content Marketing, we'll look at the tools available to help us manage these processes.

2. Optimize, Aggregate, and Curate.

Once you have an idea of the story you want to tell, the people who can tell it, and the tools that will help you tell it more efficiently, you'll need to take specific steps to give yourself the best chance for success. First, you'll need to align the right people in your organization and motivate them to help you tell the story in the right way. As you'll quickly learn, you don't have an organization that's chock full of excellent — or even motivated — writers. You'll have to optimize your content creation and aggregate and curate content from as many sources as necessary to get the best stories out.

Your new content marketing process is going to strike a unique balance between creativity, technology, engagement, communication, persuasiveness, measurement, and finance. In today's environment, it's not only important to be creative, insightful, and measured with your external communications, you must also be creative, insightful, and measured with your internal communication. As marketers, you need to be aware that never before have both external and internal communications been so closely linked. If in the words of *Glengarry Glen Ross* marketing used to be A-B-C (Always Be Closing), today's marketing mantra is A-B-C — Always Be Communicating.

In Chapter 9, Getting the Choir to Sing, we'll show you how to find great storytellers and optimize their efforts.

3. Converse and Listen.

This is where the rubber meets the road. Once you put your content out there, you'll have to stay focused not only on what you say, but also on what others say back to you — and about you.

The old cautionary cliché from our .com days of "if you build it they will come" is true here as well. But it's not enough to just publish your content. To create passionate subscribers, you'll have to share your content … evangelize it … and basically light the campfire that people will see to gather around it.

But then you'll need to listen as well. You'll need to be prepared not only for the conversation that comes from your published content, but also for the groups that form and the stories that are told beyond the bounds of your marketing. You'll need to be aware of those stories so that you can choose to lead them, follow them, or (quite frankly) get out of the way.

We'll go into these concepts in greater detail in Chapter 10.

4. Measure and Learn.

Measurement done right gives you benchmarks that provide insight into the effectiveness of your stories so that you might improve the results by changing the creative or the tactics. This includes everything from the old school method of just test, iterate, publish, and repeat, to using data to optimize your content on the fly.

On the other hand, measurement done wrong — and leveraged to "prove" how well or how poorly you are doing — boxes you in. In Chapter 11, we'll show you how to design a measurement process that isn't built to help you "prove," but rather to improve over time.

And that will close the loop of your process — and bring you right back to creation and management. Or, assuming you start from scratch, you can go right back to strategy and start over.

Chapter 7
Welcome to Workflow

"The creative process is a process of surrender, not control."

—Julia Cameron

"Stories don't have a middle or an end anymore. They usually have a beginning that never stops."

—Steven Spielberg

If we haven't said it enough, we'll say it one more time: the processes you put in place to manage your content marketing will be unique. Your story is (or should be) unique, and so too will be your method for telling it. Our goal with this chapter is to simply provide a framework for which you can develop a method of "getting it done." And in order to get it done, you need the following four things:

- People to do it
- Roles and responsibilities for those people to fill
- A schedule by which the tasks are fulfilled
- Rules and guidelines

Let's look at how you can approach each of these areas.

Assembling the Team, their Roles and Responsibilities

Given the size of your initiative and your organization, you may have one person — or many — responsible for your content marketing initiative; however, in general, no matter how many people actually take responsibility for the function, the following roles are needed across all four stages of the content marketing process:

The Manager — or Chief Content Officer (CCO)

At least one person in your organization should own the content initiative. More recently, organizations have been calling this a chief content officer (CCO). Kodak calls this role the vice president of content strategy; technology startup Radian6 calls it the director of content marketing (to see a full job description for a chief content officer, go to http://bit.ly/cco-jd).

This role is the "chief storyteller" for your content efforts. Ultimately, this person is responsible for executing the goals that you set out to accomplish. When content marketing fails, it's usually not because of a lack of high-quality content, but because of a drop in execution. This is why this manager may be your most important asset, even though this person may not be creating ANY of the content.

The CCO must ensure excellence in every content marketing tactic including:

- Content/editorial
- Design/art/photography
- Web resources for content
- Integration of marketing and the content, including social media
- Project budgeting
- Contract negotiation with freelancers
- Audience development
- Research and measurement

In organizations where there is no budget for a dedicated CCO, this role may be filled by the director or vice president of marketing. Many brands, including UPS, have a manager inside the company who oversees internal content production as well as the production of content by an outside agency. Although brands can outsource a wide variety of content production through outsourced vendors, it's important to keep the CCO inside the organization.

The Managing Editor(s)

The editors have a critical role in the content marketing process, and are probably the most sought after by brands today. As more brands develop content, more employees are being asked to blog and write on behalf of their companies. Unfortunately, the writing style of employees who have never created content before often leaves much to be desired.

That's where the managing editor comes in. This role, sometimes outsourced, and sometimes part of the CCO's responsibility, manages the editorial functions of the content marketing effort. These are your day-to-day content execution people. They help internal employees develop and write content, and they help external people match their writing to meet the organizational goals. The managing editor works with the employees on:

- Content production
- Content scheduling
- Keyword selection
- Search engine optimization of posts
- Style corrections
- Tagging and images

Sometimes the managing editors are there to teach, so the employees can do more on their own. They also may act as coaches, encouraging the managers, executive team, or even external writers to produce content against the schedule.

OpenView Venture Partners, a venture capital firm based in Boston, has a managing editor who oversees all the content on the OpenView blog, but only creates a very small portion of it. Nearly every employee is responsible for developing original blog posts, so the managing editor edits content from the entire enterprise.

Content Creators

Content creators produce the content that will ultimately help to tell the story. This role typically overlaps with the managing editors who are also producing content, but also may simply be subject matter experts within the organization.

For example, typical content producers include anyone in the C-suite, the head of R&D, the product manager, the customer service director, or a hired consultant. Basically, a content producer is any person who will be expected to produce content for the initiative.

In many cases, this role is outsourced when there is a lack, or gap, in resources to produce the content. It's important to note that this person does not need to be a writer (although it's really helpful if they are). In general, they are there to be the "face" or "voice" of the authentic organization. They may be interviewed for content, or they may produce a long, rambling email that is transformed into a cogent blog post.

Content Producers

Content producers format or create the ultimate package that the content is presented in. Chances are this role already exists in your organization to some degree; it is either handled in-house or by an agency. It might be a Web agency if the end product is a blog or a Web site. Or it might be a video production company if it's an original video, an animation or interface designer if it's a mobile app, etc.

Chief "Listening" Officer (CLO)

The role of the CLO is to function as "air-traffic control" for social media and your other content channels. They are there to listen to the groups, maintain the conversation, and to route (and/or notify) the appropriate team members who can engage in conversation (customer service, sales, marketing, etc.). For the content marketing process, this function serves as the centerpiece of our "listening posts." You establish listening posts so you can continue to get a "feed" of information so that you can always be ready to react and adapt as your subscribers react and change.

Where do these roles fit in the content marketing process? Let's look at this map:

Map of Responsibilities

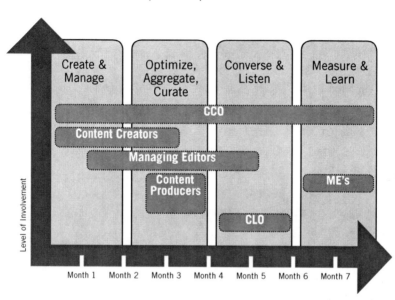

The team's map of responsibilities.

As you can see, the CCO stays engaged throughout the entire process. His or her role is to focus on the entire process and make sure that it runs smoothly and meets the goals set forth in the strategy.

The content creators are purely focused on the creation and management stage of the content marketing process. They may be fed with information gleaned during the measurement and insight phase, but their time is squarely dedicated to creating. After all, they almost certainly have other jobs.

The managing editors play an equally important role during the creation and management phase and also shepherd the content through the optimization and aggregation phase. This role may also play into the conversing and listening phase, especially as they work to make sure content is meeting editorial, SEO, or other guidelines; however, their role lessens as the content moves out into the "live" environment and is consumed.

The content producers are almost exclusively focused on the optimization and aggregation phase, as they design, format, and produce the content in whatever end form it will take.

The CLO focuses on the Converse & Listen phase. In some cases, they will actually conduct the conversation that ensues – but more likely are the "ears" of the organization. Their job is to quickly and efficiently route the conversation to the appropriate part of the organization.

Each role shifts as the process goes forward, and the percentage of time or attention that each person spends is allocated accordingly. If you look at this mapping as a part of your initiative, you can begin to envision how the workflow for the team might have to be allocated, especially given the volumes of content, the velocity, and how much external communication will be necessary.

That brings us to our second piece of developing the process.

Chief Content Officer (CCO) Magazine

CCO Magazine is the only magazine dedicated to the chief content officer. To see a sample of CCO and/or subscribe, go to http://bit.ly/CCOMAG.

The Editorial Calendar — Mapping the Story and Channels to Dates

The editorial calendar is much more than just a calendar with content assigned to dates. A good editorial calendar maps our content marketing initiatives to the personas, the engagement cycle, and the channels that we use.

In general, your editorial calendar will be a spreadsheet document that contains the following items:

1. A prioritized list of what you are publishing based on the story map you've developed. This may contain existing content, content that will be redesigned, content that will come from partners, or content yet to be developed. It is an inventory.

2. Assigned content producer(s) and/or editors responsible for the content. Here you name the people responsible for producing the content. If you have multiple editors, you identify them as well.

3. The channel(s) for the content. A listing of formats and channels targeted for the content. For example, you may have an article that will be delivered as a PDF on your Web site. You may want to identify if you will also deliver pieces of that content through a blog post, a tweet, an eBook, etc...

4. Meta data. The amount of meta data that you want to include in your editorial calendar is really up to you. You'll probably want to include tags for important aspects of the content such as "target persona" or "engagement cycle" so that you can make sure you're balancing your editorial to your overall goals. You may also want to include columns (or tags) for things like content type (e.g., white paper, video, email) or even SEO keywords, legal status, etc.

5. Dates for both creation and publishing. These include the dates that the content is due to the editor, along with target dates for publishing. These should be mapped to your story map.

If you work for a larger organization, you may want to include workflow steps such as legal, fact checking, or proofreading, or other elements that will affect your content creation and management process.

As you begin to assemble the elements you want to have in YOUR editorial calendar, remember that it's a management tool. Include only the elements you need to facilitate YOUR process. For example, if all you have is a small corporate blog for your business, there's no reason you need to overcomplicate your editorial calendar. Simply keep a spreadsheet of the story ideas — mapped by schedule to the larger story you are trying to tell and the engagement cycle — and use it to help guide your process.

One of the main benefits of having a tight editorial calendar is that you can couple it with measurement. As you roll through the timeline (your story map), you'll be able to see how the story is building (or resonating) with your audience. This can help you develop more interesting topics and avoid those that aren't resonating.

Organizing the Editorial Calendar

There are several ways you can organize your editorial calendar. For example, you can use separate spreadsheets for the different time periods (e.g., week, month, quarter, year) — or you can separate the time periods by tab within one spreadsheet. The method you choose is entirely up to you and your work style.

Let's assume that you'll have one spreadsheet for the year — and that each tab will be a month. Across the columns you might have:

a. Content title

b. Content type

c. Engagement cycle target

d. Pillars of content (or category or section)

e. Person responsible for creating

f. Date due

g. Editor (if necessary)

h. Channels

i. Meta data items

j. Publish date

k. Status (perhaps indicated by green, yellow, or red)

l. Notes (e.g., legal, compliance, review date, or other)

m. Metrics (e.g., comments posted, retweets, Facebook likes, pageviews, downloads, etc.)

Finally, as separate documents — or even tabs within your editorial calendar — you may want to include "brainstorming" elements (e.g., ideas that are under consideration or new stories that come up during the process). The editorial calendar can be a great tool for capturing creativity as well.

In the end, your editorial calendar will most likely become the most frequently used tool in your process. And whether it's a combination of documents, a single spreadsheet, or just a monthly email that you send to your team — the key is that it works for you. In the end, whatever helps to facilitate your process and keep you on track is the best editorial calendar format.

Developing the Editorial Style Guide

As a kid at camp, did you ever play the "continuing story?" That's a game where, while you're sitting around the campfire, one person starts with a sentence. They might say, "Once upon a time there was a giant gorilla that terrorized a city." Then, the next person adds a sentence, and so on and so forth, until it just can't go any further.

Usually, the story takes some wild turns — and it ends up having absolutely nothing to do with the original sentence.

Content marketing is just like this game, only now you have the responsibility of managing not only the people as they produce content on your behalf, but also teaching and leading them to respond to the content coming back from an engaged subscriber base.

Certainly, the editorial calendar will help you govern the timing of your stories as you map content to your story map; however, you'll also want to develop an editorial style guide as a tool for your content creators, editors, and producers. This editorial style guide can also develop into a social conversation style guide (aka, a social media policy), which will provide guidelines for how people should respond and converse.

As more people start "telling the story" of your brand, you need to be sure that they have the right tools and training to properly communicate your brand's voice. You also need to police them to make sure they are keeping to that voice. Like the continuing story, it's easy to let tone, quality, and style slip bit by bit — until the story is way off track. This is where your editorial style guide will come into play.

Developing editorial guidelines can be quite simple. Chances are, if you have any brand guidelines, you're well on your way there. But as part of the editorial process, you'll want to identify some things that may not be in there. Here are some key things to include:

a) The overall tone and voice of your content marketing. Use what you developed during your story mapping to help you with this.

b) The average (or maximum) length of pieces developed. For example, you may want to limit blog posts to 300 to 500 words.

c) Branding guidelines. How to refer to the company, product lines, individuals, etc.

For grammar, style, and word usage, you can also choose to conform to guides such as the Associated Press Style Guide or the Chicago Manual of Style. In addition, many content marketing strategists — especially those focused on the Web — are using the Yahoo Style Guide (http:// styleguide.yahoo.com/).

Establishing the Social Conversation Style Guide

In addition to your editorial style guide, you'll also need a separate set of rules and guidelines (and perhaps even styles) for how you'll manage the conversation that your content marketing will generate.

As you learned in Chapter 6, with the JetBlue example, ensuring that you have a model for what to say — as well as one for how to respond to something that is said to you — is extraordinarily important.

Governing social business has become a popular topic. In 2011, Jeremiah Owyang of the Altimeter Group put out his "Pragmatic Approach To Social Business." (http://bit.ly/pragmatic-approach) Chris Boudreaux has been talking about the topic for some time at www.socialmediagovernance.com. And last year, Gartner Research came out with its "How To Govern Social Media" report.

Many of the conclusions are similar:

...put somebody in charge of it

..."velvet gloves, not iron hammer" management

...guidelines and processes ...

When you develop a process for your content marketing, you want to do it in a way that ensures creative, out-of-the-box thinking in the most "human" way possible. Just as we don't want to let chaos rule the day — so too do we want to avoid the robot legalese that disengages our subscribers.

Quick example: we are huge fans of Jon Stewart. *The Daily Show* is one of the best written television shows on the air. It's amazing how every single day (well, okay, except for Fridays), despite how quickly the news moves, they manage to stay relevant, focused, and, most of all, hysterically funny.

Stewart appeared on Terry Gross' NPR show Fresh Air for a 45-minute interview where he discussed the operations of *The Daily Show.* Gross was asking him about the grind at *The Daily Show,* and how they managed the creative process. Stewart responded by saying how surprised he thought the audience would be by how regimented it all is. He said:

"I'm a real believer that creativity comes from limits, not freedom. [With] freedom, I think you don't know what to do with yourself. But when you have a structure, then you can improvise off it and feel confident enough to kind of come back to that."

That's an incredibly important lesson to us as content marketers as we develop guidelines and processes for our conversations. If we set up our processes — our content marketing editorial workflow — with a strong emphasis on governance, we can then improvise off of that governance. In short, we have rules so that we know when we're breaking them.

So what are our rules of engagement?

You'll no doubt have a debate in your organization about whether it's better to keep things more "free form" or to keep things very tightly "buttoned down" when it comes to allowing the team to respond to conversation generated by content. And if you're in an industry heavy with compliance (e.g., government, financial, healthcare), there may be very good reasons for keeping it extraordinarily tight. No matter what the setting, though, conversational style guides can help any organization be more successful.

Let's be clear: in the abstract, marketing rules, workflows, and guidelines are simple. It's very easy for consultants or team leaders to develop rules. You simply crack open PowerPoint, draw some boxes and arrows, color them in, copy and paste them into pretty Word documents, save as PDF, and say "revel in the genius."

But in the real marketing world, developing rules of engagement and workflows is HARD. It involves office politics, workarounds, compromises, difficult personalities, and consequences for a lack of adherence. What should happen when the product marketing team takes the content marketing Web site and slowly bleeds it into an advertising-filled promotional marketing hot mess? What's the consequence when a product manager shoots off his mouth and insults a prospect on a blog response?

In short — for most marketers — rules and guidelines and processes suck. It's in our nature to want to be gunslingers, and make it up as we go — and to improvise. Hell, that's where we really earn our money — right?

But NO rules? Well, that's probably not going to fly for very long. Wouldn't you rather have a rule that was broken than somebody who just "made it up?"

On the other hand, it's not a good idea to try to govern every single thing an employee can and can't say.

Put this into the agenda for one of your content marketing meetings and watch people physically shudder. Both of us have been in some organizations (especially larger ones) where just the mere mention of conversation rules is enough to completely shut down any and all social media efforts. I mean why bother — right?

But, of course, you should bother. The key is to create balance (and we're guessing you already know the culture in your organization well enough to know what it is) in the rules. Then, you can choose whether you're going to break the rules and for how long — or implement them right out of the gate — or phase them in with a smaller team first.

There are no hard and fast rules about what your conversation style guide should have in it (although you can find a sample at www. managingcontentmarketing.com). We've seen people agree to the rules with a handshake. We've also seen documents containing hundreds of pages detailing every rule and guide. But the real point is to develop a conversation style guide that provides your team with a set of answers to issues … something that empowers them … something that "frees" them from anxiety and doubt when it comes to the question of "how should I answer this?"

So with all of that said, a conversation style guide should contain three sections:

Online communications guidelines — What are the fundamental principles for online communications? Do you have any principles that already exist (e.g., guidelines for corporate communications, brand guidelines, principles of the organization)? Do you have policies in regard to things like transparency, protection of privacy, respect, and responsibility? Is there (or should there be) overriding online communications principles?

Are there legal disclaimers that should be applied on your blogs and/or social Web accounts? Will any third-party disclaimers be necessary (i.e., these opinions are my own)? If so, is that part of the overall communications guidelines? Who is responsible for creating and managing these disclaimers?

Do you have any brand guidelines for how people should conduct themselves on the social Web, especially in terms of tone, accuracy, transparency, and consideration? Is there one voice? Or many? Is controversy okay? Is politicial discussion okay? Current events?

Should you explicitly say, "Don't reveal confidential information?" What is your disclosure policy when dealing with "influencers?" What will it be for employees who want to tweet, blog, or otherwise publish under your name?

Individual responsibilities and behaviors — Can employees post anything they feel, so long as they use "good judgment?" Or must they always get permission? Or are they forbidden to say anything, under any circumstance, unless they are told to?

Do you have privacy concerns? What about mentioning other

employees by name? Customers? Constituents? Partners? Is it always okay, or okay with permission, or never allowed?

What are the personal responsibilities of the content creators and producers?
Will they be held responsible for anything they write or produce?

Who will respond to negative or very sensitive responses or other content?
What is the escalation process for conflict resolution?

At home (or on their own time), do employees need to get permission before starting a blog or personal page that mentions the company? Do they have permission to use trademarked material (e.g., logos) in personal content?

Is it okay for people to personally comment or respond to mentions of the company they see in other blogs? Should they?

Disaster recovery and crisis management — What process is in place if disaster strikes?

What if a provoked or unprovoked takeover happens on one of your channels — or if things were to get wildly out of control? What should the process be?

A typical answer might be, "senior manager will notify all direct social Web managers to cease all communications until further notified."

The key is to keep things clear so that everybody knows exactly what's going to happen.

The risk of no rules at all is clear. But just remember that if the rules are too tight, your story will come off like a government documentary. Consider these three rules (of more than 50) that we took from the social media policy of a large company.

- Do not access any of your personal social networks while you are working at COMPANY.

- In your privacy settings, especially LinkedIn, block your connections from viewing your network. Your connections should not be allowed to see COMPANY customers and/or partners that we do business with.

And our personal favorite …

- You must obtain the E-team's approval before responding to any social media comment made on any COMPANY social media channel.

Now doesn't that sound like a peachy place to work? How many do you think actually comply with #2?

Don't be tempted to fall back on that most clichéd of all corporate trampolines, "When in doubt — set a rule for it."

Apply Practical Wisdom

Try applying the lessons of practical wisdom to the idea of social media policy and governance. We've put it in place in several companies and have seen it have real success in creating positive social Web business practices.

If you're not familiar with the idea of practical wisdom, it's an idea that originally comes from Aristotle's Nicomachean Ethics — or a concept known as phronesis. It's what Aristotle called the "master virtue." Put simply, it's the ability to use reason in situations that have a moral dimension to them.

(There's also a wonderful book by Barry Schwartz called *Practical Wisdom: The Right Way to Do the Right Thing* that we can't recommend highly enough.)

Basically, the idea is that in any effective social media strategy you need rules. This is especially true of late — with new guidelines and compliance regulations starting to emerge within finance, healthcare, government, and other regulated industries. You have to have rules that deal with legalities, privacy, etc. And let's be frank — if you don't have some guiding policies for your content, your legal team will be almost unbearable to deal with (rules will keep both sides sane).

But the real success is not in giving the team a set of rules, but the trust and power to reason and act beyond them. Sometimes we chalk this up to just letting the team use "common sense," but it's really getting to the heart of making the business human.

We have to realize that there is no amount of rules that we can put in place that will prevent disaster from happening. There is no governance plan that will be water tight enough to not allow savvy employees from ingeniously figuring out ways around the rules. And the tighter we hold, the greater the temptation to find those cracks.

So what to do instead?

Set intentions with your social media policy. Yes, make rules where necessary, but understand (as in Jazz music) that the rules are meant to be bent. They are meant to be reasoned and we assume that smart people will apply practical wisdom. They will have the morality to do the right thing — and the skill to know what the right thing is.

Last year in New York, Barry Schwartz did a TED talk on practical wisdom. Search for it on Google because it is really worth 23 minutes of your day. In it he sums all this up by saying:

"To love well and to work well you need wisdom. Rules and incentives don't tell you how to be a good friend, or a good parent, or a good teacher. Rules and incentives are no substitute for wisdom. Indeed, there is no substitute for wisdom. It not only gives us the ability to do right by others, it gives us the ability to do right by ourselves."

Chapter 8
The Tools of Content Marketing

"A worker may be the hammer's master, but the hammer still prevails. A tool knows exactly how it is meant to be handled, while the user of the tool can only have an approximate idea."

—Milan Kundera

In college, Robert's college roommate used to hold up a giant screwdriver and say, "This is the only tool I'll ever need." And, he'd hammer nails with it, open boxes with it, open beer bottles with it (yes, college was like that). It was everything he needed. Sadly, the same can't be said for all the different tools you need to manage a successful content marketing process.

The tools you really need are there to help facilitate the process you've come up with. That's why this chapter comes after the one on "human processes." If you get the human process right, you'll have already developed the most important tool. And the technology tools that will make your life easier will start to really define themselves.

Depending on your content marketing strategy (and your size and budget), the number, type, and robustness of the individual tools you will need may vary greatly.

For example, if your entire aim is to produce a new blog, then a simple implementation of WordPress (or a similarly hosted system) will be just fine. But if your strategy is more holistic — or you work for a larger organization — you may need to look at more "enterprise-class" Web content management solutions.

When we discuss tools that are appropriate for the content marketing process, we are speaking in terms of the TYPE of tool you need to build your content marketing engine. To that end, the suite of tools that will typically support this engine consists of:

- **Tools to manage content and publish it to your channels.** This goes beyond simply updating Web pages, sending email newsletters, and/or providing an easy way for non-technical people to update your social media channels — we're talking about tools focused on the core functions marketers need from digital content: tools that will help you publish search engine-friendly pages, manage landing pages, easily segment marketing lists, send relevant emails to your subscribers, build forms, and publish any content to any destination in any format.

Web content now lives beyond the bounds of your Web site, and any tools you can find that will help you create and distribute content that can be shared beyond your Web site will be useful. Tools here run the gamut — from simple content management tools such as WordPress, Joomla, Drupal, and Movable Type — to enterprise content management systems (CMS) such as Sitecore, Tridion, and Interwoven.

- **A conversion management and/or data capture and management tool.** These tools give you the ability to create registration forms or landing pages, and capture the data from those forms in a central unified data model. This data should, like the content that is managed, be able to be published or exported to any format at any time. For example, leads should be able to be exported to Salesforce.com (or your preferred customer management platform). Examples of tools in this space include simple online form data capture tools such as Wufoo or Google Docs, to sophisticated lead management and nurturing tools such as Marketo, Eloqua, and Manticore.

- **A content optimization and targeting tool.** We're not talking about a "personalization" tool (which has been represented in many types of solutions), but rather a tool that gives you the ability to segment elements of your content to your personas based on explicit or implicit sets of criteria.

Your goal should be to deliver the right message to the right person at the right time. For example, a B2B marketer that sells to both IT and marketing wants to ensure that once a visitor has identified himself as a target persona, that he is given optimal messaging that delivers a relevant message. Or a B2C marketer may want to enable a set of videos that are optimized for different mobile devices. The online marketing engine tools must enable you to deliver content based on customer segments. Sample tools in this space include simple A/B testing tools like Google's Website Optimizer, to sophisticated testing and targeting tools such as Adobe Omniture, Autonomy Optimost, and CrownPeak's Web Content Optimizer.

• **Tools for managing/listening to the social Web.** There are plenty of tools here to help facilitate publishing and listening to the social Web. You may opt for a simple dashboard like TweetDeck, something more "team-based" such as HootSuite, or full sentiment analysis using tools like Radian6 or Sysomos.

• **Measurement tools.** You're probably already using tools like Google Analytics or Adobe SiteCatalyst to measure your ongoing marketing and Web site activity, but you may want to examine more sophisticated options for looking at content consistency and accuracy such as Magus Active Standards. There are also features in your CMS that you can use to continually examine the quality and staleness (age) of your content, and update activity.

If you can, consider systems that are best of breed and that work together, rather than giant software suites. You need to be able to launch small experiments in a timely manner. Chances are, you already have pieces of this solution in place, and there's no reason to replace what you don't need to. You may have a Web CMS, or a lead management solution, a content optimization solution, or an aggregate analytics solution. Content marketers need to employ a solution that is able to mold itself around any existing solution to close the loop on your online marketing engine — without requiring you to start anew. Further, you need to be able to roll out new programs without added or extra support from technology specialists.

Best Practices for Selecting Technology Tools

Selecting and implementing a suite of content marketing tools is a project within the larger process. It has a beginning, a middle, and an end. But you're helped because you have your strategy so tightly created and formulated. You know exactly what your process will be, so selecting content marketing tools becomes relatively straightforward.

Certainly considerations of how you'll break down your content and manage it beyond content marketing will come up and you'll need internal buy-in. Then, your selection project will typically fall into the following four-step process:

1. Decide and buy
2. Implement and integrate
3. Manage and maintain
4. Upgrade and enhance.

This process can be applied for each tool individually, or as a more comprehensive acquisition. Each step has its own challenges, deliverables, and requirements.

1. Decide and buy.

Once you've decided on your process and you have internal buy-in, consider developing an "official" document that will explain the tool's implementation project and your desired outcomes in detail. This project definition will be your requirements document as you gather all of the desired outcomes and new capabilities, and start to map them against a set of features, functions, and services that you'll require from your chosen solution.

Many larger organizations choose to outsource the project definition phase to consultants with either vertical expertise and/or previous implementation experience. For example, a CMS implementation is rarely limited to just content marketing requirements, so you may want to examine the content management needs more holistically as you look to acquire a tool.

In general, the goal of the project definition is to outline:

a. The scope of the project — what this project will entail (which divisions, which platforms/channels, etc.).

b. The business goals of the project — what the business will achieve from a business point of view, and how you will measure the success of the selection and management of the tool (refer back to your content marketing strategy for those goals).

c. Key assumptions being made — what key assumptions need to be made and dependencies outlined in order to satisfy the deliverables?

d. Key people involved — who is participating and what are their roles?

e. Functional business requirements of the project — these are the key benefits, not specific features (e.g., easier to publish content more atomically to different formats, or to publish search engine-friendly content — not "XHTML-compliant output").

f. Functional technical requirements of the project — keep these high level for now, but capture any critical items (e.g., must be Microsoft-based, or must be able to scale as site and content marketing needs grow).

g. Cost and duration of the project — your budget and timeline.

Once you've developed the project definition, there will typically be a natural prioritization in terms of the features, functions, and services that your organization will require. Separate these, both in the document and in your selection process, into "product features" and "services/vendor" requirements.

For example, you may have a strong need for implementation services because your technology team has limited bandwidth, or, in the case of some smaller organizations, is non-existent; or perhaps you have strong product feature requirements (such as workflow or custom measurement needs) because you are in a regulated industry.

Developing the short list
Next it's time to develop a short list of potential solution providers (perhaps four or five) and develop a Request For Proposal (RFP).

There are a number of analysts and resource Web sites available to you online in order to develop a short list of vendor candidates for all kinds of content marketing tools. Go to www.managingcontentmarketing. com for some guidance on this if you need it.

RFP overview

Try not to get too focused on granular sets of capabilities in a feature/ function matrix. Unless you have very specific feature needs, you are unlikely to get actionable information from these feature-by-feature comparisons. Most likely at this point, all of the vendors will check the "yes" box. Instead, develop "groupings" of features from the general business requirements you defined in your project definition, and have the vendor comment (in a paragraph or two) on their ability to meet these specific sets of prioritized features or benefits.

Then, once you have your short list of solutions, consider developing a One-Month Review Cycle for the top solutions. Below is a sample schedule for a vendor review cycle:

Week 1: RFP goes to four of five vendors on a short list. The RFP should spell out anything in particular that you'd like to see demon-strated during a meeting, which will be scheduled that week.

Week 2 or 3: Online or in-person demonstrations with all vendors on the short list. If possible, all stakeholders should see all demos. At this point, you may start eliminating vendors based on capabili-ties shown in the demo.

Week 3: Proposals due from all remaining vendors. Keeping the proposals mercifully short is a key instruction. Remember, a 20-page proposal from four vendors is 80 pages of reading for you and all your team members.

Week 4: Decision and contract negotiations with chosen vendor.

If that sounds too simple, it's because it's often made far too com-plex. In general, if you do your homework on the front end — and make sure that your short list of vendors are qualified — any of them should be able to handle the "technical functional" require-ments of your project. So the decision will (and should) come down to the following business intangibles:

- Which solution will meet all my business needs the best?
- Which solution will be easiest to use, assuring high adoption among our content marketing team?
- Which solution will enable me to get up-and-running the fastest?
- Which solution provides me with the best support and ongoing service?
- Which solution will scale as my needs grow and change — facilitating change instead of impeding it?

2. Implement and integrate.

Entire books have been written about best practices associated with implementing software into your organization, so we certainly won't try to capture all the detail here. In addition, the implementation and integration will differ greatly depending on the type of solution that you've chosen (e.g., email vs. CMS vs. analytics — or installed vs. hosted or commercial vs. open source). But as you put together your project plan consider the following helpful safety tips:

a. Check your time before you send the check — before you choose a vendor, make sure you get an estimate and/or commitment on the implementation time line and that it meets your business need.

b. Don't try to boil the ocean for launch — again, this is a new process in your organization. You will assuredly not get it exactly right upon your first launch. There are always unforeseen obstacles and more often than not something will be left out. So accept that now, and don't spend weeks and weeks trying to capture every little feature. Phase your launches and get the key functions up first. Your tools should be flexible enough for you to make easy and fast corrections along the way.

c. All content should have an owner — there should always be someone responsible for the quality and placement of all the content. As we discussed in Chapter 7, this can be different people for different articles, assets, sections, or pages on the Web site or even social media, but all forms of content need to have an assigned owner responsible for making sure it is up to date and correct.

d. Simplify your life, your workflow, and your approvals — resist the urge to use the technology tools to "herd the cats." If your workflow process is too complex or cumbersome, be prepared for resistance to adoption. The main goal is to get these new tools to help speed the process, not be a hindrance to it. Keep it simple to begin with, and then add restrictions as people either violate something, or need to be managed.

3. Manage and maintain.

Choosing the right tools is important, but along with your more comprehensive strategy, developing the right plan for services and support of those tools is even more important. For some reason, services often take a back seat to product selection during the early phases of deciding what tool to implement and when budgets are often set. So here's a word of caution: don't get so caught up in the bright, shiny features of the tools that you forget that someone has to manage and support everything.

The two pieces of successful management are the 1) implementation, and 2) ongoing support and maintenance. You have to get them both right, but the more neglected of the two is, of course, support and maintenance. The consequences of failing to implement correctly are clear: the software doesn't work, is clunky, or buggy — or all three. However, the consequences of failing to manage and update the system are much less clear, but over time are just as severe.

Usually, the internal IT group is chosen as the answer to this challenge, but it can certainly be a problem to develop and maintain expertise in the software application and find free developer time, especially when rapid changes are required over and over again.

The bottom line is this: Don't skimp on building post-launch services into the project plan and budget as you start your software selection and implementation. Define the players and responsibilities in the immediate post-launch "tweaking blitz" and for the maintenance, upgrade, and modification program. It's not the glamorous part of the project, but assuming you've picked a tool that will be flexible and scale with you, success in the support and maintenance phase will determine how long the tool lives and how successful it is in the months and years post-launch.

4. Upgrade and enhance.

So you've launched your suite of tools. You've trained your end-users and you have a hold on your maintenance challenge. The tools are all working together as a content marketing engine, and they're flexible enough to handle ongoing system enhancements and changes. Now you can think about upgrading and enhancements to your project. This is where the process really begins all over again — and where putting good thought and work into that more comprehensive process really starts to pay off.

The key here is to approach these upgrade and enhancement phases as just a mini-version of how you approached the initial project; you can go right back to the beginning and start the process all over again. Create an addendum to your project definition document — and move on from there. Hopefully, you can skip the selection of tools because you've chosen one that will grow with you.

Choosing the right tools will truly strengthen your business. They will not only create efficiency for the content marketing process, but also (depending on your business) provide you with a number of opportunities to create competitive advantages, revenue opportunities, and new avenues for customers and partners to communicate with you.

You're an expert in your business — and you shouldn't have to become an expert in software in order to be successful. Consider working with subject matter experts who can become a core part of your team and help you through this process.

Figure Out What's Right for You

To be sure, the steps you take today are the first ones. And as a process, there is room for mis-steps. Of course, the earlier you start, and the smaller the steps you take, the more room you'll have to make many more mistakes than you might otherwise. As you formulate strategies and select tools, you should start at best practices — but don't end there.

Your customers don't care what this is called, or how you manage your content marketing process, or what your internal capabilities are. They will just know that your content exists, and how your organization deals with that content will be the indicator of whether it helps you or doesn't.

As Yogi Berra once said, *"You've got to be very careful if you don't know where you're going, because you might not get there."* (Yes, it was one of his famous flubs.) In managing your content marketing, you may not be completely sure of where you're going and that's okay; if you've developed a process and a strategy, at least you'll know you're ready to be there.

Chapter 9
Getting the Choir to Sing

"Every writer I know has trouble writing."

—Joseph Heller

B elieve it or not, once there is agreement to start content marketing, the biggest objection and fear isn't about budget, success, or even reaching goals. It's "how are we actually going to get people to write this stuff?"

In fact, 4 out of 10 marketers surveyed in the 2011 Content Marketing Institute "B2B Content Marketing Benchmarks, Budgets, and Trends" study said that "producing engaging content" was their biggest challenge. More than 20% cited "producing enough content" as their biggest challenge. And, finally, 18% cited finding the budget to produce content as their biggest challenge.

One of the most critical reasons for this is a lack of a process and clarity around the story that needs to be told. Here are some of the typical challenges:

- We dive right into the middle of this process, thinking we know how to be thought leaders in our industry, or how to produce compelling content that our audiences will care about.

- We assume (oooh, there's that word) that we know exactly what content needs to be produced.

- We assume that it will be quicker to "write it ourselves" than to get thought leaders in our business integrated into the process.

- We let our subject matter experts run wild with their ideas — and then spend far too much time cleaning it up for messaging, brand, and story.

- We take it for granted that our internal subject matter experts will produce content with a velocity that we can depend on.

- We never really understand the value of bringing in outside content.
- We simply don't "get" that the content needs to revolve around the core needs of our customers.

Now, the good news is that you have this book and you've developed a clear strategy, a set of guidelines, and a wonderful story. So let's get this story moving by assembling your team. Let's beat the drum to help your content creators actually produce and fuel your content marketing engine.

Finding Your Team — Your Writers, Your Sages

How many people in your business are good writers? In fact, how many on your team even have a formal marketing education? The answer to the first question is probably "not many." If the answer to the second is also low — you're not alone. In fact, corporate giant GE found out in 2006 that only 34% of its 5,000 marketers had any formal marketing training at all.

Is it any wonder then that the other departments in your organization have absolutely no clue as to what you mean when you start throwing around terms like positioning, branding, engagement, impressions, or value proposition? Do eyes glaze over when you start spouting your own acronyms like CMS, SEM, or PPC?

In their book *Groundswell: Winning in a World Transformed by Social Technologies*, Charlene Li and Josh Bernoff say:

"Throughout corporations around the world, employees are connecting on internal social networks, collaborating on wikis, and contributing to idea exchanges ... they tap the power of the groundswell of ideas among the people who know best how your business runs, your employees. It's a little scary to put this power in the hands of your workers. It doesn't fit into a nice, neat org chart. But if you want to run faster and smarter, you ought to take a look at it."

Finding the best people in your organization to participate in your content marketing initiative may be self-evident. If you have a passionate C-level executive, or VP of marketing, or (in some cases) employees who are called "evangelists," the challenge of finding people may seem quaint.

But in some organizations, both large and small, finding the best people — especially the ones who can tell the story you've come up with can be more challenging. They may be hidden away, so make sure you look closely. You don't want to miss out on a wonderful opportunity. You know that quiet guy who sits in product marketing? He might not say much, but when prompted, he may be able to write rings around anyone you've ever seen.

Quick example: a small software company (about $2 million in annual revenue) that we worked with started a thought leadership blog. The original idea was that the authors would come from the C-suite. The CEO would cover strategy, the CMO would take the marketing angle, and the CTO would post technical information. It worked for about two months before "life got in the way" and the editorial got bogged down. So, as an experiment, they opened it up to product development. The results were amazing. Two of the product engineers (highly technical) produced a passionate piece on why the company was so great to work for. Then, a sales rep posted a piece about best practices for buying their type of software. And it exploded from there. The company switched the story it was telling and rebranded the blog. And with almost no prodding — it's now a point of honor to get a post published on the blog —it's a thriving content marketing initiative for the organization.

See how a "happy accident" can uncover untapped passion and talent within an organization? What are some of the things you can do to start looking for these people in your company?

Well, as Li and Bernoff suggest, internal collaboration environments are a great way to get ideas flowing. Whether it's a virtual collaboration environment like a Wiki or a discussion board, or a simple in-person brainstorming session, the key is to start fostering an environment of collaboration around content — and then drawing from the well of your passionate employees.

Who can instigate this flow? If it's not you (and it should be), we're sure you can identify some of these people within your organization. You know — the ones who are ready, willing, and able to tell your story at the drop of a hat ... the ones who you're already afraid will say something "rebellious" and you wonder how you're going to keep them governed. That's a good problem to have.

And that brings us to our second challenge ...

Educating Your Team — Getting Them to Understand Your Message

It's a fast business we're in these days — and when we're moving this fast, it can become easy to forget to keep our internal circles as engaged as we'd like our customers to be.

It's important to market your content marketing plan internally – even if you're a small organization. You'll want to ensure that the entire team understands what you're doing – and why their efforts are important. In other words, you want to get them invested.

There's a great book on this topic titled *Light Their Fire: Using Internal Marketing to Ignite Employee Performance and Wow Your Customers* by Susan Drake, Michelle Janette Gulman, and Sara Roberts. In it, they say:

"Employees must buy your message before your customers do. They must understand why your product or service is important, know what it can do for customers, believe in its integrity, and be inspired to make it even better. Employees have to understand where the company is headed and why."

There's a reason why writers on TV shows meet weekly to discuss the finer parts of the larger story. Everybody needs to understand the larger story arc, and where the marketing is headed. Now, if you're just producing a blog, this might be as simple as having everybody in a meeting understand the content marketing strategy and the editorial calendar. But for a larger initiative, you may want to create an internal content plan that gets ALL of the stakeholders invested in your initiative.

You're a marketer. You already know how to do this. You'll never find a friendlier audience for your content than you will with your fellow team members. Employees want to be motivated — and they desperately want to be on your side. That said, here are some considerations for developing an internal marketing plan:

- **Segment your audience and develop your personas.** Yes, it's here, too. Define WHO in your organization you want to talk to, and HOW you'll talk to them. Make sure you understand what their present level of understanding is. Chances are you don't want to speak to the IT guys the same way you speak to the sales team.

- **Set your goals.** Understand your priorities and create a map of which groups (both up through management and down through the organization) need to be informed, how quickly, and to what end. How will you measure? Can we make this fun? Not in some weird corporate way — but really interesting? For example, a contest to see who can produce the blog with the most comments? Maybe even have a competition? (In fact, Compendium, a blogging platform, and ExactTarget, an email marketing platform, once had a three-month blogging contest where vacation days and bragging rights were on the line.)

- **Set the tone and the messaging.** Here's the part where you can get creative. What are you trying to communicate — and what do you want that desired effect to be? Again, you already know how to do this.

- **Determine your channels (i.e., how you'll reach them).** Would an all-hands meeting be the best choice? Or should you have an online community Wiki or an e-newsletter? Should you have individual meetings? A Webinar series?

- **Measure.** You didn't think you were getting out of this part, did you? Make sure you have a process to measure how you're doing. Assign a champion in each department to give qualitative feedback — but make sure you have some quantitative measurement as well. It could be surveys or other methods depending on the size of your company.

You can have the most efficient, engaging, and effective content marketing program in the universe, but if your internal team isn't invested in it, it may not fail, but it certainly won't be nearly as success-ful as it could be.

In the end, it's definitely preaching to the choir — but as Scott Adams says, *"When the choir isn't singing, they're just a bunch of people standing around in colorful robes."*

Which leads up to our next step …

Encouraging Your Team — Optimizing Their Efforts

One of the critical stages of the content marketing process is the optimization, aggregation, and curation phase. This is where the managing editors really earn their money. As we said in the beginning of this chapter, it's highly unlikely that you are blessed with a team of good writers and/or storytellers.

Transforming a person's passion, expertise, and thought leadership into one or multiple elements of your story can be difficult. We can't tell you how many times we've heard one of the following sentiments after we've nailed down the content marketing strategy:

- Our CEO doesn't write — in fact, no one in our organization writes (almost certainly not true).

- Our CEO can't write (okay, maybe this one's true)

- How are we going to get all this content created — I just don't have the resources (almost always true to an extent)

Here are some ways to overcome these challenges:

Capture in their format of choice — Some CEOs love to write, but most CEOs like to talk. If it's a challenge to get your C-level executive to produce thought leadership content, capture their thoughts in a different format. Interview them using Skype, and record the conversa-tion. Your managing editors can turn that into other content market-ing pieces (e.g., blog posts, white papers, etc.). Or, if the content is good enough quality, you can use it in the captured format. Or, if they can't really write — but they're willing to just type an email — tell them to just write a long email to you.

When you're at industry events, be sure to capture photos and video on your phone. Mix and match them with pieces of content that you may or may not produce. Maybe the video gets used in a customer interview.

Another thing you can do is just sit down with the person. If there's a product manager who is shy, or doesn't feel like he can write 500 words on a particular topic, interview him. Take them to lunch and record the conversation. Again, re-use that content in multiple formats.

Help them tell stories — Many times when you're talking with executives about writing and creating content, you have to begin by simply teaching them what "writing" is. The act of writing is just transferring what's in your head to words. As the famed sportswriter Red Smith used to delicately put it — all you have to do is "sit down at a typewriter and open a vein."

Of course the real magic in turning writing into a story or something worth reading happens in the editing process. Relieve your team of their worries, and assure them that the copy will be "polished up" during editing. Then get them rolling, by offering the following tips:

- Write it out. Just write blind — get it out. Writers are usually surprised by how much structure and genuine goodness comes out by just opening up and not letting their mental "editor" get in the way. Tell your prospective contributor to just spend half an hour typing out his or her thoughts.

- Storyboard it out. If they're having trouble getting anything going or opening up, tell them to just visualize what they want to say and write down key phrases, or concepts, onto sticky notes. They can even draw what they're thinking onto sticky notes. This is an especially great way to organize thoughts for a longer piece.

Help them become aware of content opportunities — In one technology company we worked with in the past, much of the customer service happened through back and forth email. When we did an initial content marketing audit, we realized that a large portion of blog and article content was happening through direct customer email. It took only one customer service rep to notice this, and now the entire organization looks at the content they create every day as part of their business. Now, customer service reps, as well as sales reps, are more routinely aware if one of their emails should be used as an FAQ on the Web site or expanded upon in a blog post.

Determining if You Need Outside Help

Okay quick — how many marketing consultants does it take to change a light bulb? There is no shortage of punch lines here. *"It depends — how large is your budget?"* Or — *"We don't know — they never seem to get past the requirements stage."* Or, here's our favorite (maybe because we made it up) — *"Four: one to change the bulb and three to blog how Seth Godin would have done it."*

Okay, jokes aside — once you've developed a content marketing process and you've explored the capabilities (or bandwidth constraints), you may determine that you need to outsource some of the work or all of it. After having read Part 1 of this book, maybe you even felt overwhelmed and asked yourself how you can hire a consultant to tackle that phase.

Let's break it down into two areas you may want to seek help with.

A Consultant to Help Set the Strategy

This is your story, but sometimes you need help telling it.

If you're struggling with the strategy, consultants can help bring out your unique story — the one you want to tell — and help you set the stage to tell it. If you think that sounds like a good idea, then it may make sense to bring in an outside consultant.

A good consultant will:

- Bring the experience of previous engagements and help you avoid the pitfalls that are inevitable in setting any new large effort

- Help uncover your unique conversation

- Devise the execution plan

- Reset expectations among the team, especially where there is internal disagreement about the details of how it will all get done.

"But isn't that why we pay the marketing department?" you may hear — or even ask yourself. In other words, "it costs too much."

This is a common objection for consultants in general. In fact, calling an engagement "strategic" immediately puts the business user on the defensive. Shouldn't you be the "strategic" ones?

Frankly, a content marketing consultant should not be hired to set marketing strategy because it's your story. The consultant is just there to help you tell it and teach the organization how to do something new, or more efficiently — or (by nature of the fact he or she is being paid), force the effort to the top of everyone's priority list.

For example, Robert has a personal trainer. He doesn't have Robert do anything he doesn't already know how to do, but he pushes harder than Robert would push himself. Consequently, he prioritizes exercise in between sessions so that he doesn't lose ground and "disappoint" the trainer. That makes the trainer worth his fee, which can be a valid reason to employ a consultant.

"But our business is unique. How can this consultant help us?"

When an organization says "our business is unique" what they're actually saying is "our content is unique." And, as we've discussed previously, this is true across EVERY organization.

Part of the content marketing process is *finding* that uniqueness. Bringing in someone who doesn't know ANYTHING about your business can shake the trees for some things that hadn't been previously considered. Additionally, learning from a consultant about how someone outside of your industry did something can provide invaluable insight about differentiating from the competition.

On the other hand, sometimes it's helpful when the consultant does have experience in your industry. For instance, previous knowledge of what is and isn't appropriate in regulated industries like finance and healthcare can expedite the consulting process.

An experienced consultant with the right set of expectations should be able to help sort through the weeds. They've done this before many times. They know the pitfalls, the best practices, and ways to navigate the politics of recruiting others in the organization. They can provide sanity checks for getting things done, plan how roll outs should be phased, suggest what kind of content velocity is appropriate, and, ultimately, uncover the realistic opportunity for the content marketing effort to succeed.

As marketers who have been on both sides of the marketing consulting relationship, we know how good and how bad the experience can be. No matter which side of the table you're on, paying attention to the details will prevent your content marketing engagement from winding up as a punch line.

What to Look for in Freelance Writers

Once you have a working strategy, you may find that you need help developing ongoing content — or that you need additional content producers to keep up with the velocity. In either case, you may need to develop a case for "getting it done."

How do you go about finding good external content contributors? Should you look for a good writer and teach them your business? Or should you hire someone who knows your industry and teach them to write? Here are a few tips to consider:

- **Expertise is helpful — but not a deal killer.** Given the choice between a good writer with a personality that closely matches your organization (but short on industry expertise), and an industry veteran that knows how to write but with whom you can't stand to be in the same room with — go with the personality. Chemistry and personality are things that are entirely hard to change; research is a skill that can be taught — passion isn't.

If you and your freelance content producer don't have good chemistry together, the relationship will go nowhere fast. And while it might be a strategic advantage to bring in an industry "rock star" to get your content some attention (and there are great reasons to do this occasionally) — unless there's a great personality fit, be very careful that you don't wrap your story into theirs and get lost in the middle.

- **Hire right — copywriters, journalists, technical writers, oh my!** Because you've spent so much time on your strategy and your process, you should be very aware of what kind of writer you're looking for. Understand that copywriters work very differently and have very different sensibilities than do journalists. If you're looking for someone to write blog posts for you, a copywriter is probably not your best bet. On the other hand, if you're looking for someone to beef up your persuasive call to action for all the great white papers you're putting together, then a great copywriter may be exactly what you need.

• **Develop the right business relationship.** Understand what the elements of your business relationship will be and make them clear. For example, will it be one content item per week — and your writer will be paid a monthly fee? If so, how will you handle months that have 4 1/2 weeks? Will there be an extra post that week? Spell out the invoicing and payment terms. Given the size of your organization, you'll either need to make clear the invoicing and payment terms — or understand what the writer needs.

Also, be clear on expectations. At this point, you should know your velocity and how long and how detailed the content needs to be. There should be no surprises like blog posts suddenly becoming 300 words, when they're supposed to be 500. Or content themes going wildly off topic.

Here are some of the things you'll need to communicate to your freelancer:

• What content they'll be producing and where it falls on the editorial calendar

• The goals for their specific contributions

• What expertise or other third-party information they'll need access to (will they be interviewing internal people, bringing in external information, or reworking your existing material?)

• Your budget

• The number of revisions for each piece.

Even though you'll be able to find some outstanding freelancers, resist the urge to fill your entire strategy with them. It may seem easier to just relegate all of your content production to a team of writers that you can control — but it's ultimately a counter-productive strategy. A great freelance consultant can help you fill gaps in your content production machine, and even "fish for you"; however, you should strive to learn and be capable of telling your own story.

Ensure the Right Fit

In the end, a good content marketing freelancer or agency — no matter which role you bring them in to fill (e.g., managing editor, content production, etc.) — needs to be an extension of your marketing department (really an extension of your entire company). To do a proper analysis of your needs, you should undertake a process similar to the one you used to select your technology tools (described in Chapter 8). This will help you determine your business and process requirements, but keep in mind that cultural fit may be the most important element of all.

Chemistry isn't just important to have with vendors — you have to have it with your audience as well. To build chemistry you need to engage in conversations with them and build relationships. Which leads us to our next chapter ...

Chapter 10
Talk the Talk and Listen In

"Doing business without advertising is like winking at a girl in the dark. You know what you are doing, but nobody else does."

—Steuart Henderson Britt

"Seek first to understand, then to be understood."

—Stephen R. Covey

Well, you've made it this far. You have a process for creating compelling content. Your content marketing engine is humming, you have your team producing engaging, shareable content — and you're ready to watch the results just start to flow. But here's the problem.

Creating quality content by itself is not enough.

The entire reason that you built a business case, put a strategy together, built your team, developed a workflow, and hired freelancers or an agency is because you have a story to tell. Now it's time to share that story. There's a funny joke that says the only difference between a stand-up comedian and a crazy person is an audience.

Digital marketers have been steeped in the belief that the reason we create content is so that it will be there when people search for it. We've been told that we need to create content for the "long tail" and that Google will magically find this content. And because we've largely created this content to raise ourselves up for search, we think once we've created this content that — yes — they will come.

It's not true.

Your content is now a conversation. It's a story that needs an audience to respond to. So, yes, go out and create great content. Be the leader in your industry because you consistently share value. BUT, share it. Find out where your customers are hanging out and be there. That means online, offline, and even in print. Get involved in authentic conversations.

You simply cannot be the trusted leader or content partner without actively being a part of the conversation. This is easy to say but hard to do (and this is incredibly difficult for large brands).

As with any conversation, there are two parts — talking and listening. Both are equally important. The "talking" is sharing our content so we can start to drive toward the goals we've set for ourselves. We call this the "marketing of the marketing." This may be through social media, through a paid placement in a print magazine, or through a PPC search campaign to direct people to our content. Whatever form this takes, at the end of the day it is a concerted effort to draw people into our conversation.

Next comes the "listening" part, where we not only engage in the conversations that we start — but also listen in to the conversations that are happening outside the bounds of our content. Here's where we identify new opportunities for us to create new content and new conversations.

The Importance of Marketing the Marketing

Walk by a Williams-Sonoma store in the fall, and you're likely to be drawn in by the overwhelming smell of cinnamon — or cooking garlic. As you walk in, you'll see people gathered around a stove receiving instructions on how to cook from an experienced chef.

Now, of course, Williams-Sonoma doesn't give free cooking classes out of the goodness of its heart. This is content marketing at its finest. Wouldn't you like to purchase the special maple rolling pin? You know, the one that transforms the dough of your apple tartin into a thin disk of delectable pastry without stretching, tearing, or overworking it? Oh, that's right — I thought you might.

But what you didn't see when you walked in was the small fan — blowing the smell out into the mall. Yes, they're actually blowing the aroma out into the mall to draw you in.

In September 2010, software company Vocus, along with Brian Solis, principal at Altimeter Group, released a research study titled, "What Makes An Influencer" that examined how marketing execs perceive "online influence." From a content marketing perspective, here are three things that stand out from a "marketing the marketing" perspective:

- When asked to rank "why you follow a person or organization," more than 60% claimed "because they share relevant content" as the primary or secondary reason.

- Respondents were also asked to choose a single action that would be the most important action a person or brand could take to increase their influence online. Half of them said, "create compelling content."

- Then (and very interestingly) almost two-thirds (57%) of those polled said they would "pay an influencer" to help drive actions or outcomes. And of those, maybe not so surprisingly, the biggest groups were "advertisers" and those responsible for "search or SEO."

Sometimes it's easy for us to forget that we can use paid media to drive engagement with our content. We get so focused on the "acquisition" metric that we only use paid media to drive people to something that immediately can be translated into dollars.

Quick example: We were working with a B2B company recently, and one of the things they found was that while using PPC advertising to drive people to "talk to a consultant" provided a lot of leads, those leads didn't ever convert into customers. They were simply tire kickers looking for free advice. So we switched to a PPC campaign that drove people to engage with content. We used keyword strategies to drive people to important blog posts, white papers, Webinars, etc.

Now each piece of content had a call to action itself; it may have been asking the reader to engage in additional content, or to request a demo at that point. The result was (as you might expect) lower conversion rates for some content, and higher ones for others. But the proof in the pudding was in sales. Total sales went up, because we started attracting more serious buyers. That drove the cost-per-acquisition (CPA) for PPC down, and as a result, search engine marketing was more effective. Additionally, we started to get better insight into which content resonated the best with which type of buyer and applied that knowledge to the editorial calendar.

That's just one example of the many strategies you can use to get your audience to engage. It only makes sense that if you're going to create all this compelling, thought provoking content that you have to share it and market it extensively — and advertise it as well.

In short, you need to buy a couple of fans to make sure the wonderful smell of what you're cookin' makes it out into the mall.

Listening In — Setting Up Your Listening Posts

To this point, we've discussed two things related to setting up your "listening posts." One of the main team members we identified was the chief listening officer (CLO). You'll remember that their role is to function as the "air-traffic controller" for the social media and other content channels. They are there to listen to the groups, maintain the conversation, and to route (and/or notify) the appropriate team members who can engage in conversation.

The other tool we identified during the workflow process was the social media policy guide. This governance model is what helps you give freedom to the people who are "listening" to the conversations you are generating. You need them to respond and create more content, and more conversation. Therefore, you use your social conversation guide to make sure they are doing that safely, and within the confines of the story you want to tell.

There are two aspects of the listening process. The first is to make sure you respond quickly and decisively to the (inbound) conversations you're generating. This includes, but isn't necessarily limited to:

- Responding to blog post comments
- Responding to questions or comments submitted through your site or social media channels
- Engaging on your social media channels
- Chatting with people during online events
- Answering emails.

Next there is the proactive (outbound) listening through the channels where we aren't necessarily engaging in conversations, but where conversations may be taking place without us. This includes, but isn't necessarily limited to:

- Monitoring keywords on social media channels (e.g., Twitter, Facebook, LinkedIn, Google+)

- Monitoring sentiment through the social web (e.g., blogs, comments, social channels)

- Monitoring our brand name or personnel through keyword searches.

Let's look at how you can establish a process for listening in and routing conversations:

1. Define and align your goals.

In general, social Web monitoring will include a broader set of goals than just your content marketing. For example, your PR team may be using social Web monitoring to monitor brand mentions in order to mitigate any public relations disasters. Or, your customer service team may be in charge of monitoring the "support" email address for product support issues. Or your sales team may be using social Web monitoring almost like listening to a "police scanner," watching for the mention of keywords that may indicate an opportunity. Or if you're a smaller business, all those people might be you.

In many cases, the conversation that is coming both in AND out of your organization is content. For example, once a blog post is produced, your audience will now have the opportunity to respond. Just understand that they may not stay on the exact topic that you want them to. Your CLO needs to monitor that and understand if a response should be:

A) Ignored, deleted, or responded to

B) Routed to someone for additional action.

Whatever your situation, the key is to align your content marketing goals — and the conversations that are happening — with your overall goals. The last thing we want to do as marketers is open up a new content marketing program (let's say it's a blog) and have it explode in our face as customers swarm all over it to complain about our product.

Quick example: A consumer products company had launched a new blog as part of its Web site strategy. And, while the content was really directed and positioning the company as a "thought leader" in its industry, there were problems with the product. The blog started to fill up with comments and complaints about the product. The marketing people didn't really have any alignment with the customer support group, and chose to ignore or gloss over the comments. Pretty soon it became so bad that there were more customer complaints coming into the marketing blog than into the customer support community. The company had to shut down the blog before it even had a chance to succeed.

The lesson is to ensure that as you roll out your content marketing programs — and the listening programs that will accompany them — define and align your goals with other parts of the organization as well.

2. Identify actions for triggers.

As you define and align goals — and start to establish your listening programs — there will be triggers (something happens that we need to do something about) and actions (what we should do). The number of triggers and associated actions can be large, but here are a few to illustrate the point:

Trigger: We need to know immediately if someone says something bad/good about our brand on our blog or on our Facebook page.
Action: It it's bad, route it to our social media manager for response. Or offer a customer service channel to resolve. Or (and this is sometimes okay) ignore, but note.

Trigger: Someone is talking about a need for our product on Twitter.
Action: Route this to outbound sales or marketing so they can send a standard social media communication.

Trigger: We've reached an X threshold of negative sentiment on this particular topic, or on this particular piece of content.
Action: Route to marketing (or the CLO) for action.

Each of these actions can be counted and included as part of a KPI associated with the content or content marketing program.

Let's use our story from above as an example of this. That story actually ended differently than we led you to believe. The company didn't actually shut down the blog because it became overwhelmed. Actually, because they caught this trend early — and they were tracking each customer support complaint and routing it to customer support for follow up — they started to notice a few things:

A) They tracked the number of customer support issues coming through the blog; and because the number was growing, they actually added customer support as one of the pillars of content into the content marketing strategy (they re-wrote the story).

B) Because of this trend, the company decided to integrate (as calls to action) direct links to the support forum from within targeted blog posts.

These two actions started driving much more traffic into the customer support form, and started to decrease the amount of customer support calls they were getting. The content itself became searchable, sharable, and helpful to their customers. Over time, they decreased their customer support costs substantially.

What started as a blog directed solely at driving sales through content marketing became (secondarily) a content marketing initiative with the goal of decreasing customer support costs.

See how it all starts working together?

3. Recognize that inbound conversations are different than outbound conversations.
Remember that there are big differences in the way that you treat

inbound and outbound conversations. An inbound conversation — whether it comes in the form of an email into the organization, a comment on a blog post, or in a support forum — is the equivalent of the customer walking up to you and saying, "I have something to talk with you about." Yet even if they're saying something "nice," this is NOT tacit permission to use their comments as a public endorsement.

However, if someone writes very nice and lovely things about you on their blog, that's the invitation for an outbound conversation and that IS an endorsement. And you should feel free to link to it, point people to it, and generally feel pretty darn good about it.

The same holds true for negative conversations — when someone posts a genuine problem or issue on your Facebook page. The Facebook interface may NOT be the best place to try and resolve that issue. Create a process that allows for the person to vent (for your customer's and your brand's sake) in a more private environment. Then, once it gets resolved, make a decision about whether to publicly acknowledge that fact.

4. Make sure your CLO knows and loves your social media policy.

Your CLO must be thoroughly familiar with your social conversation guide and be able to communicate it throughout your organization. Don't let a flare up of some trolls on your Facebook page throw the whole company into chaos. It's very likely that something will derail your story at some point in time (e.g., a product mishap, an unhappy customer, a rude customer service person, or a scandal involving your CEO). Having a solid social conversation guide and a disaster recovery process will help you mitigate any other mistakes you may make by responding too quickly — or not quickly enough.

5. Use your ears to flow the data.

Your listening posts are like an organization's ears. In fact, you can think of it as you do your own ears. The human ear is divided into three main parts: the outer ear, the middle ear, and the inner ear. The outer ear is responsible for helping to locate the origin of a sound — whether it's behind us, in front of us, or above us. It also helps to funnel and focus the sound into the middle ear. The middle ear contains the auditory canal which ends at the ear drum. This is where the sound waves are converted into electrical impulses and sent along the auditory nerve to your brain. The inner ear contains the semicircular canals which function more for the purpose of equilibrium than for actual hearing.

Think about that structure as you organize your own listening process:

The *outer ear* of the organization – can be managed by your CLO. With the obvious exceptions (and you'll know what they are), the role of the CLO will just be to watch for triggers and take the initial action to route comments or conversations to the appropriate people. The CLO may also track and follow through to make sure things are being "heard," but his or her primary role is to listen, locate, and route.

The *middle ear* of the organization is each department where responsibility for action may lie. These are the people who react, who actually convert the conversation into an insightful reaction to continue moving the conversation forward.

The *inner ear* of the organization is upper management, or people who don't provide much "hearing" function, but provide the brand balance. These are the people in the process who help us make sure we take a strategic approach to our response. This may be your legal team, or even your C-level managers who need to help balance your conversations back to your audiences.

There are a lot of ways you can relay these conversations throughout the organization, but emails or IM alerts are most common. You can also set up dashboards or reporting structures through your content management system if you need more sophisticated types of notifications and approvals. In general, the more fluid the better, and as discussed in the goals section, it makes sense to track these things over time. Just like managing a good conversation, managing a good listening post involves knowing:

• How quickly things are getting responded to

- How the information is flowing through the organization
- Whether the subject matter experts are engaging directly, or are they just answering — and then the answer is massaged by marketing?
- What is happening after conversations take place — what follow-through tools are being used to ensure the loop is closed (e.g., email, phone calls)?

6. Monitor what's important.

Beyond the conversations that your organization will start, you can expand your proactive monitoring to keywords, hashtags, or even (through specialized software) "sentiment analysis." But remember it doesn't always have to be about you. You may decide that monitoring competitors and their weaknesses is a good thing. You may decide that monitoring sentiment about your partners is a good way to keep track of any disasters that may be looming. You may decide to monitor campaigns, or even temporary keywords based around holidays, specials, etc.

Get creative with your monitoring — you may be surprised at what business value you can provide by just keeping your ear to the ground.

7. Match the tools to the strategy.

What kind of listening do you want to accomplish? If you need to monitor in different languages, look at more sophisticated toolsets. Or if you need to track compliance, or integrate with your CRM systems, make sure you understand those business requirements before going in. Then go back to Chapter 8, and apply the tool selection process here as well.

Talking and listening are both necessary for building relationships. No matter what your goals may be (e.g., to build subscribers, to build relationships with influencers, etc.), you have to have a two-way relationship with your target personas in order to be successful.

Whatever you do, don't use listening as a way to extend your reach. It will be tempting to use monitoring like a security camera, reacting to every single movement that you see. But after the third or fourth time out in the dark chasing that single, elusive mouse, you'll find that there are far more pressing challenges to deal with.

Chapter 11
Measurement: Developing Your Pyramids

"Say you were standing with one foot in the oven and one foot in an ice bucket. According to the percentage people, you would be perfectly comfortable."

—Bobby Bragan

Did you open to this chapter first? Come on, did you? By far the question we asked get the most at the various conferences we speak at is, "How do I measure results?" It's actually the corollary to the first question we mentioned in Part 1: "How do I show ROI?"

For marketers, measurement has come a long way; it's to the point now where analytics and measurement tools are built into almost every technology we use. It doesn't matter if it's Web content, email campaigns, social media, or all of it — we can measure just about every single thing we do these days.

In fact, this explosion of capability has created a huge transformation in the depth and level of measurement. Today, it's no longer enough to just sit back and watch the statistics and hope they continually go up and to the right; we need to put a process in place that parses that data and derives true insight.

As Avinash Kaushik says in his book *Web Analytics: An Hour A Day:*

"You know you live in the world of key insights analysis when you realize that every piece of data you look at drives action — and not just action, but action that adds to whatever bottom-line outcomes that your company is trying to achieve for your customers."

To Kaushik, this means measuring both the "what" and the "why." This is incredibly important to us as content marketers. Looking at the quality of engagement, and understanding the sentiment and resonance of our content are critical pieces of our measurement strategy.

In this chapter, we're not going to try to explain how analytics work, or why they are important to your business. We'll leave that to the experts like Kaushik. Instead, we're going to examine how to develop a framework — specific to content marketing — that can help you prepare the measurements that matter.

In the wrong hands, a notebook full of statistics is a disaster waiting to happen. Put simply, your analytics data doesn't convert customers. Never once has a graph showing more visits or telling a prospective customer about increasing conversion metrics — or sharing the percentage of conversions vs. bounces — made any marketing campaign more successful. It will always be your compelling, creative content, which helps you build trusted relationships, that ultimately generates sales. Content — online, in print, and in person — is what converts customers.

Data is only important if you have something relevant to measure. Ask yourself this question: Would you rather tell your CEO:

A. Web traffic doubled from 20,000 to 40,000 visits per month — but sales remained flat.

or ...

B. Traffic decreased by half — from 20,000 to 10,000 — but sales doubled.

Our guess is that you went with B (now if you can also say that marketing costs are flat and revenue doubled, then you just earned your bonus for that quarter).

Of course, in order to get to B you absolutely need to have your finger on the pulse of a great number of metrics. And establishing a great base of measurement ensures that you can measure EVERY-THING you need.

Measuring everything you need, but reporting only what is important is key in creating an environment that allows for innovative experiments and the ability to "fail fast." Ideally, you want to create an "analytics pyramid"— a structure of measurement that allows you to use a large variety of metrics to create specific insight for managers. In a moment, we're going to show you how to build your "analytics pyramid," but before you start, consider the following:

1. Know what's important.

As you develop your process for measuring content marketing, it will be really important to give quality feedback to the participating team members. Begin by talking through the priorities with your CEO, as well as all the participants in the process. Each will have a set of measurements that align with their individual goals — and also feed up into the larger goals.

What you should end up with is a hierarchy of measurements. In other words, as you get down lower in the organization, you'll have many reference points. And, as you move higher (toward your CEO and the executive team), that dashboard may have no more than 3 to 5 basic metrics that provide the KPIs that you need in order to show success. As it pertains to your content marketing, your CxO is only going to care about the following:

- Is the content driving sales for us?
- Is the content saving costs for us?
- Is the content making our customers happier, thus helping with retention?

The reports you show to your CxO need to answer these types of questions, or why show them anything at all? Content marketing is all about developing content that maintains or changes a behavior, so that is the focus.

As you move down the pyramid, you add more and more of the things you're measuring, and these are less and less important to actually provide reports on. By the time you get to the bottom — these may be numbers that only you or members of your team care about.

2. Always be learning and making subtle changes.

Measurement is constantly shifting — and this is key as you build your analytics pyramids. You will definitely change methodology for measurement as you move forward; however, if you focus your strategy on making subtle changes to individual methodology — these changes should not have an effect on how you report your 3 to 5 KPIs to your CxO. Your CxO does not need to know that the definition of Web page visit has changed in your reporting, or that you've split your Facebook channel into two – and therefore your "likes" have dropped by 50%. You should always be learning how those subtle changes affect your numbers so that when you report your KPIs, you are confident in them.

3. The numbers aren't always "the way."

Interpreting analytics is frequently not as straightforward as a "science." Sometimes, as a marketer, you can — and should — do things that fly in the face of the numbers, either from a branding perspective, or some other business or creative function. For example, there was a national telecommunications provider that we worked with where the CEO loved the lower converting creative, and hated the higher converting version. It wasn't a lot lower — but lower nonetheless. We talked it through. Guess which one was kept?

4. Keep in mind the real purpose of analytics.

When determining whether you should report on something, the question should always be "what is the action we can take based on the result of this reporting?" Every report should have a point of insight that drives you to a creative action — either changing content, design, or business strategy to adapt to new experiments to test.

5. Budget for success AND failure.

Don't take on measurement or try one tactic unless you have permission to fail. You will succeed and you will fail. And if all you're focused on is a hard ROI for every single marketing tactic, you've already lost. This is one of the main reasons for not reporting every analytic measurement to your CxO. This gives you the freedom to fail and experiment — all while staying focused on the larger goals.

Building Your Analytics Pyramid

First of all, recognize that it may be easier to create an analytics pyramid for each of the goals you are trying to achieve. Let's go way back to the goals we identified when we built our business case for content marketing. Remember, these were some of the goals we identified:

Build brand awareness or reinforcement
Create more effective lead conversion and nurturing
Increase customer conversion
Optimize your customer service
Increase customer upsell
Create brand subscribers

So let's say you're putting together an initiative to build more brand awareness for your company, and also optimize your pipeline for a more effective lead conversion process. (For this goal, you have decided to create a thought leadership blog. Additionally, you will leverage some of your social media channels to feed readers into that blog. Finally, according to your story map, you're going to build your audience over the first six months, and start introducing calls to action around month seven.)

Here is how your pyramid might look:

GOAL PYRAMID

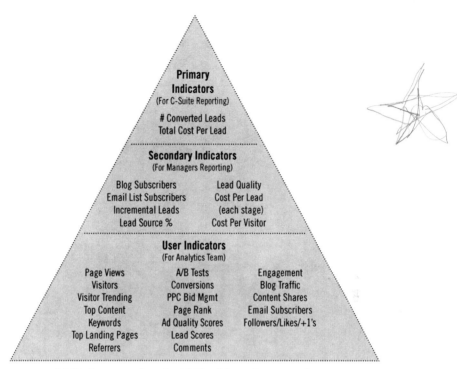

GOAL: Increase Leads 10% with no increased cost

Step 1: Segment your pyramid. Segment your pyramid into three divided lines. The bottom, widest part of the pyramid will be your USER INDICATORS. This will be the "long list" of various numbers that you're tracking. These are the metrics that are audience-based, and are meant to measure activity. They will almost certainly overlap your other pyramids in various ways. You will slice, dice, add, subtract, and change these metrics on a frequent basis. Many of them may only exist for a short time — or be very specific to one campaign.

The second level of the pyramid will be your SECONDARY INDI-CATORS. These will be the metrics and KPIs that you associate with team members — and specific processes that help you reach your goals. These are generally what we think of as "short-term goals." These metrics (or KPIs) may change based on campaigns, or other needs, but in general are specific to the process that feeds the goal they support.

At the top of the pyramid are your PRIMARY INDICATORS — or the KPIs for the goal. These metrics will be very few in number and will be the dashboard that you present to your manager or CxO. These metrics change very rarely, if ever, and are fed by the insights, interpretation, and data from below. The goals are what you REPORT.

Step 2: Map the segments. Your goal in this example is to "increase the number of converted leads by 10% without raising costs," and you've created a new thought leadership blog to help you accomplish this goal.

There are a few ways you can get to that number. You can either improve the conversion rate of the existing number of leads by 10%, or you can *increase* the actual number of leads by a percentage so that the number of converted leads naturally goes up by 10%.

So to build your PRIMARY INDICATORS, you'll only want a handful of numbers in that top dashboard:

- Number of converted leads by week/month/quarter
- Total cost per converted lead by week/month/quarter.

Boom — that's it. Those two numbers are the only KPIs (for that particular goal) that matter to the CxO.

Then, for your SECONDARY INDICATORS, you may want to monitor a number of metrics; these will give you great insights and help your team improve the process in order to reach your goals. Examples include:

- Engaged blog subscribers vs. goals
- Email list subscribers vs. goals
- Total number of leads by week/month/quarter
- Incremental leads from the new blog
- Lead source (e.g., organic search, Twitter, Facebook, etc.)
- Lead quality (conversion rate by entry into the engagement cycle)
- Cost per visitor
- Cost per lead at each conversion layer.

Applying these metrics to your story map will enable you to start making strategic decisions about the goals you've set for the blog.

For example, based on your story map, you may not have a goal of generating actual leads until month seven. So the only SECONDARY INDICATORS you will be tracking for the first six months will be "engaged blog subscribers" and "email list subscribers" — for which you may have incremental goals. Once you start to learn in month seven what percentage of subscribers will turn into leads, you will have insight into whether you need to expand, change, or modify your strategy to meet your top-level goal.

Lastly, you have your USER INDICATORS at the bottom. These are the day-to-day metrics that will help you understand and get the insight to improve the process of your secondary indicators. Examples include:

- Number of visitors to the blog
- New visitors vs. returning visitors
- Pageviews on the blog
- Number of blog comments
- Blog subscriptions
- Conversion rate from subscribers to leads
- Number of shares through social media (most shared posts)
- SEO metrics for keywords
- Twitter followers
- Facebook likes
- Sentiment analysis (social media listening reports)
- Social media reports (both internal and external)
- Blog comments and responses (qualitative)
- Most popular blog content/category
- Time spent on the site
- Bounces (how many bounce from the site)
- Visitors by source (where the visitors are coming from)
- Cost per visitor (if we're paying for visitors through other media)
- Persona measurement (if we're attracting our targeted personas).

The purpose of these metrics is to help improve your process. If you find that you're putting a lot of time into Facebook — but are not getting any visitors or subscribers out of it — you can alter our strategy and experiment with other social networks.

User indicators will be your day-to-day finger on the pulse of how your content is doing. Because you've taken the time to map your blog content to your personas and your engagement cycle, you'll also know where these visitors are coming into the engagement cycle.

For example, if you start to notice that you're getting some traction with blog content (you're not getting many leads, but they are very well qualified leads), then you'll know that you should optimize your content to focus on increasing the conversion percentage. If, on the other hand, you start getting a lot of visitors to your blog at the very top end of the engagement cycle, you will know that you need to increase the TOTAL number of leads to get to your goals — and you can change your strategies accordingly.

Step 3: Create the insight and reports. Beyond mapping the various metrics to the parts of the analytics pyramid, the next step is to put this data into a useful format for your team. In general, every metric should have an insight and action associated with it. If it doesn't, reconsider whether you actually need to measure it.

Then, consider a weekly or monthly report for your immediate team on the user indicators — and insights from these to actions. Map the user indicators to your team's responsibilities and get them invested in the outcome. This doesn't mean they are solely responsible for improving the numbers, but it will show them where their expertise will help. For example, you might map these as follows:

The Project Manager
- Number of visitors to the blog — What can we do to increase this number?

- Page views on the blog — How many pages are visitors looking at? Should we change the site to be easier to navigate?

- Blog subscriptions — Are we marketing the blog well? How can we get more interested people to subscribe to our blog?

- Conversion rate from subscribers to leads — How are our calls to action working? Do we need to A/B test new landing pages and/

or persuasive content?

- SEO metrics for keywords — What are our top keywords for this blog — and how are we doing with getting them included? Do the content producers and editors know that this is important?

- Social media followers/likes — Which channels are developing and resonating for the blog? Which are sending traffic back to the blog?

- Visitors by source (where are the visitors coming from) — Which sources are producing the most traffic, the most engaged users? How do we get more content onto these channels?

- Cost per visitor (if we're paying for visitors through other media) — If we're paying for media, how do we drive down the cost per visitor, or optimize the number of visitors we're getting from our paid media?

- Persona measurement (are we attracting our targeted personas) — Mapping back to our goals, our personas, and the engagement cycle mapping, are we getting who we're looking for?

The Editor

- New visitors to returning visitors — Are we generating loyalty? How should we change the content to help with this?

- Number of blog comments — Are we asking for comments? Are we constructing conversational posts?

- Number of shares through social media (most shared posts) — Which content is being most shared? How do we develop more content like this?

The Content Producers

- Most popular blog content/category — Whose posts are resonating the most? What are we doing right? How can we produce more on that topic? What can we do better?

- Time spent on the site — Are our posts too long? Too short? Informative enough? Are we cross-linking enough to our other posts?

- Bounces (how many visitors bounce from the site) — How do we make our content more interesting upon first glance?

The Chief Listening Officer

- What is the sentiment analysis (social media listening reports) for these initiatives, our brand or our product?

- What kind of metrics are we producing from social media activities ("Likes," "+1's," "Followers," Engagement)

- Are blog comments trending up or down? What is the general tenor of the comments?

- What are the results from CLO follow-through? For example, how many passed comments have resulted in a sale?

Connecting the Dots

As you build more of these analytics pyramids to your goals, you will start creating a sophisticated measurement and content-driven organization. If you spend the time to do this the right way, you will have A LOT of tools to answer some extraordinarily complex questions about your content marketing as well as your overall marketing strategy.

You can take it even further by mixing and matching measurement with your planning to get some extraordinarily detailed insight. For example, you can map your personas and their engagement cycles to your most popular content and channels and build a report that shows which marketing channels are performing the best in relation to the engagement cycle. You may find some interesting things, for example:

- Social media channels are producing the most qualified leads

- Cost per lead decreases significantly when you use Google AdWords to drive white paper downloads instead of email subscriptions

- You're attracting way more of Persona One, but Persona Two makes up a much higher percentage of your qualified leads.

What do those things mean? Well, that's where you'll earn your stripes. For example, given the above, should you create more content to attract more of Persona Two — or should you work on better ways to more effectively convert Persona One? Or both?

Another point to keep in mind during all of this is that your goals and pyramids will quickly start to proliferate and overlap. Now that you're creating customers, you'll need to start keeping those customers — and upselling them. And that brings us to the last part of our measurement strategy ...

Creating Subscribers is a Creative Marathon, Not a Quick Hit Sprint

At this point, your CxO knows you're in control. You've got clear KPIs and you own a content marketing process; it may or may not be focused on selling your product, but it's certainly focused on clear goals. As a result of that, you're now content-driven to match buyer behavior and you're committed to a content marketing process that focuses on an idea — not selling a product or service. You have a process around the management of your measurement. Put simply, you're built to improve your process, not prove anything. And, remember that this is a new process, and one you've not previously employed. In other words – it's still a game – but it's a different game.

Consider that the average MLB game is 2 hours and 50 minutes long. The average NFL game is 3 hours and 7 minutes long. So give or take 17 minutes — or about 10% — they are roughly equal in length. However, consider that the action in a football game is only about 15 to 18 minutes of that time — and that the game is timed. Even in the case of a tie, there is only one more 15-minute period in which to come to a winning conclusion. In a baseball game, the ball is almost always in play, and theoretically the game could last days — as there is no "set" time that the game must conclude.

That's 15 to 18 minutes of all-out sprinting, leaping, bone crushing athleticism vs. a long, strategic, mindful process interrupted by the occasional sprint — that has no artificial end.

Consider also that a baseball season is 162 games vs. 16 for the NFL, and that during the playoffs, baseball teams must win multiple games against the same opponent (vs. in the NFL when whoever wins on that particular day advances).

Now we're not arguing which sport is better, but traditional marketing, for the longest time, has been treated by most businesses like football. Every game can be won or lost — and if lost, can spell doom for the entire season. The risk-reward for every game is incredibly high as the difference of one win can mean the difference of going to the playoffs or being relegated to the bottom of the pool until next season. As a player, one wrong fall, one mistake in a game can mean that you're finished with a season-ending injury. It's all about trying to get to the Super Bowl — one game that will determine it all.

We've got to break out of this.

For content marketing, it's a long season. There are, and should be, many chances to fail — as long as we fail quickly, learn, and adapt to the new surroundings. Each tactic that we try — if we look at it as a game — is just one of hundreds of others that we will play. When we win, we'll feed that strategy — we'll work it again and we'll feed that success up through our analytics pyramid. And, when we lose, we'll quickly learn and adapt — maybe even within a series against the same team.

So, what does your CxO need to know?

The same thing that your CFO needs to know — it is a fool's errand to treat content marketing as a 16-game season. And it's impractical to think that you're going to maintain perfect ROI. You have to look at a content marketing investment as a long-term strategy to engage audiences. You must be able to experiment with new tactics. You must have a budget to fail — and you must have a longer-term view of how the marketing investment will pay off.

Marketing as a Long-Term Business Investment

Because of generally accepted accounting rules, your company will most likely require you to treat marketing as a short-term expense. It's an interesting paradox, though, when you think about what huge benefits can be derived long-term from marketing vs. some of the other things we treat as long-term.

For example, when we look at "long-term" investments such as R&D on product development and other types of research and then balance the true return on investment vs. marketing, many times our marketing investments get the short end of the stick. It's clear that at some point, we will need to re-examine marketing investments from an accounting point of view.

But that's a fight for another day — because we're certainly not going to advocate going in and arguing with your CFO about that. We've got people to engage and subscribers to create.

Rather what your CxO needs to know is that we need to treat content marketing as a long season. You need to be able to look at the lifetime value of your customers; yes, you will try things that fail, but you're also doing things to help retain these long-term, high-value customers. Remember, content marketing is an asset that can live for a very, very long time (unlike most advertising).

Your CEO also needs to know that there are intangible benefits that come from increasing content marketing budgets, and from some of the tactics that content marketers use. Some of these are hard to point a finger at, but do contribute substantially to that one metric that we all care so much about: revenue growth.

There's a quote attributed to Paul Richards, a manager for the Baltimore Orioles in the 1950s, that sums it up very well. He said of baseball (and we think you can switch it with today's content marketing) that it's *"made up of very few big and dramatic moments, but rather it's a beautifully put together pattern of countless little subtleties that finally add up to the big moment, and you have to be well-versed in the game to truly appreciate them."*

Batter up …

Chapter 12
Beyond Content & Marketing

"Do you know the difference between education and experience? Education is when you read the fine print; experience is what you get when you don't."

—Pete Seeger

"A mind that is stretched by a new experience can never go back to its old dimensions."

—Oliver Wendell Holmes, Jr.

It's certainly not lost on us that, as we move into the middle part of the current decade, many marketers we talk with are saying, "I haven't even gotten used to the idea of creating content — and now the whole world is abuzz with creating 'experiences.'"

We also hear marketers saying that more is expected of them; they're not only responsible for generating leads, but also for servicing customers. They're expected to create experiences that not only create NEW customers, but that keep the existing ones engaged and advocating.

Guess what? That's okay.

The "new" marketing funnel. (See chart on next page.)
We're looking at a new marketing funnel these days. When we're successful with a comprehensive content marketing initiative, the smallest (by numbers anyway) of our "subscribers" are usually at the middle of the funnel at the "customer" stage.

This funnel tends to imply the level of effort we're paying to these audiences. It's no surprise that, as marketers, we've paid A LOT of attention to the top of the funnel. And now that we have a content marketing engine, we have the opportunity to spend A LOT more attention to our advocates, our evangelists. Amen!

So beyond content marketing, we can start to think about content sales strategies, or content CRM strategies, or whatever we want to call it. No matter what the name, the goal is simply to move our satisfied customer to the upsell stage — and then into evangelism. Can we propel them forward with content? With conversation? Can we turn them into passionate "subscribers?"

But all of this is not only beyond marketing, it's beyond content. It's not linear. If you get anything out of this book, just remember what we said at the beginning:

Nothing that's happening here is new. The lesson learned from Web 1.0 to Web 2.0 was that good business sense needed to be applied to this new technology. And now, as Web 2.0 fades and Web 3.0 is introduced, just realize that the new platform is just that — a new platform. While it's revolutionizing the ease in which we communicate, if we don't have something valuable to say or to create — well, we still won't be heard. Forget whether these are old rules, or new rules. Today it's about getting beyond the hype and embracing the power of community and the ease of facilitating conversation — and letting the flow of the Web work for you.

The "New" Marketing Funnel

Beyond Content — It's Ultimately More than What You Say

Maya Angelou, American author and poet, once said, "I've learned that people will forget what you said, people will forget what you did, but people will never forget how you made them feel." It reminds us constantly that communication is about so much more than WHAT you say.

It doesn't matter whether it's called "customer experience management" or "web experience management"; at its heart, content marketing is about telling a compelling story. And at the heart of telling a great story is creating an engaging experience. And, at the heart of creating an engaging experience is focusing on how we evoke a feeling. And that is all made possible 100 times over today because 1) technology enables us to do it better, and 2) customers actually let us in and accept our story.

The Experience Economy: Work Is Theater & Every Business a Stage, by B. Joseph Pine and James Gilmore, is a wonderfully relevant book more than 10 years after it was written. One of the ideas that continues to resonate is in the introduction, where the authors discuss how experiences are a new source of value. Remember this was written more than a decade ago:

"Experiences are a fourth economic offering, as distinct from services as services are from goods ... When a person buys a service, he purchases a set of intangible activities carried out on his behalf. But when he buys an experience, he pays to spend time enjoying a series of memorable events that a company stages — as in a theatrical play — to engage him in a personal way."

That's incredibly important to us as content marketers as we learn to evolve. We are in the business of telling a great story. And we need to remember that, in addition to text and images and video and interactive tools, real people and real, tangible things can tell that story as well.

Quick example: We recently finished a content marketing project for a software company. They market a product that sells for hundreds of thousands of dollars. Their sales cycle is long, and (as you might expect) they touch many people during the lead nurturing process. One of the most interesting content marketing initiatives we put together was a story around the "project manager" target persona for this product and how he or she can become a "super hero."

Because of the complexity of this company's offering, there is usually a project manager for the implementation and roll out of the software. Typically this person has to manage the creation of a number of new processes, change the behavior of a number of people, and deploy a whole slew of new technology. So we created a series of workshops that would teach the project manager the "best practices" of not only how to "buy" this kind of software, but also how to successfully implement, manage, and achieve adoption in the organization. These workshops are highly valuable experiences — taught by practitioners at the software company who "know the ropes."

In addition to the project manager, different stakeholders are also brought in for different workshops; however, the project manager is always positioned as the one true super hero. He or she becomes the "go-to" person in the organization for this new process. When it's done, he or she looks like a genius. Can you guess how much affinity these workshops create between the project manager and the software company?

Now, of course, the company has leveraged these workshops into blog posts, Webinars, white papers, and every other form of content that's running through your brilliant brain at the moment. The experiences become yet another source of telling the story that this company is trying to tell—and supports what they REALLY do for a living. This company's story isn't about producing "business process software"—it's "making this particular business process disappear."

Here is the most important piece of this initiative: this company has no interest in (nor could they afford) providing a complete set of training courses on these various subjects. These sales prospects may or may not even be able to buy from them. These workshops are not designed to train the project manager on every detail of the software, or the process. Frankly, that's what the company gets paid for during the consulting and training services they offer.

No, they are designed specifically to give just enough information in just the RIGHT WAY, to make the prospect team feel good, gain confidence, and build trust with the software vendor.

In short, they're not built to truly educate. They're built to make their prospective clients stakeholders — and especially the project managers—feel ever-more confident about the big decision they're about to make.

As content marketers — when we're at our best — we create experiences that are memorable and evoke an emotion. When we can make people feel good with our text, our imagery, our videos — our story — we're creating wonderful content marketing. But let's not forget about also inviting people to our live stage — and that creating a real-life experience is just as compelling. And this not only applies to generating leads — but also to servicing customers.

Beyond Marketing — It's Also About Internal Collaboration

A few years ago, when the term Enterprise 2.0 hit the collective business consciousness, there was this breathless air of excitement. Of course, it made sense — it's like Web 2.0, only now we'll do it for servicing our customers. It's genius, right? The idea of the enterprise using content and "emergent social software platforms to pursue its goals" (to use the inventor of the term Andrew McAfee's definition) seemed, at the same time, both really familiar and cutting edge.

While the social Web has made an unmistakable mark on consumer behavior, calling it Web 2.0 has come and gone. But what of Enterprise 2.0? Well, from recent reports it would seem we're either convinced that it's still the "core part of the business application framework" (from the current E2.0 conference overview), or as "Enterprise Irregulars" blogger and ZDNet writer Dennis Howlett said when we asked him his opinion — "a crock."

Regardless of which side you fall — there's no shortage of money in the space. SuccessFactors bought CubeTree for $20 million, StatusNet picked up $1.4 million to take a Twitter-like application behind the firewall, and SalesForce.com has purchased Radian6, the sentiment analysis vendor.

So money flows, conferences launch, and panels assemble — it all feels very familiar. Cue the big swirly psychedelic video effect. We're back to five years ago. Content marketing is a brand new, hot business topic.

The idea of using content to drive marketing results had this kind of anxious anticipation. Businesses were started, books were written — and entire practices were created within advertising agencies.

The promised benefit of content marketing has — five years later — just started to transform the marketing process to engage customers, collaborate and converse with them, and share more freely across the enterprise. Compare that to the first benefits of the promise of Enterprise 2.0. Again, according to Andrew McAfee on the *Harvard Business Review* blog: "…the tools help people find information and guidance quickly and reduce duplication of work … they allow executives to realize the dream of creating an up-to-the-minute repository of every-thing an organization knows."

Realizing the Dream?

So, okay — some of that has come to pass, right? There must be real case studies of real companies doing something with content and enterprise social software. Right? Well, there certainly are, but most of them are like the old content marketing case studies from 2007/2008. They're kind of like the old Jeff Foxworthy "you might be a redneck" bit: If you've deployed a Wiki or a highly customized version of Share-Point with content and link-sharing — you might be E2.0.

What's the challenge? Is it a lack of the right features in the tools? Are there adoption challenges? Is it integration? Or is it as Dennis Howlett said when calling E2.0 a "crock"—the case that "the circus has moved on with analysts and vendors now trying to co-opt the social CRM moniker, pulling in bits of the E2.0 social media detritus so it looks good"?

Whatever the reason, it's not lost on us that this content marketing process naturally lends itself to building internal "subscribers" as well. Many organizations are beginning to think about applying a content marketing-like strategy to solve internal communication and collabo-ration challenges. One disturbing trend, according to ContentWise, is that over the last 8 years, the gap between internal content marketing and external content marketing continues to grow. Now, just 21% of content marketing initiatives target internal subscribers. We believe the time is now for that course to reverse. It is now that we need to focus on "our" people in order to properly execute an external content market-ing program.

If E2.0 survives as a concept, look for this to happen. Content marketing practices can and should be used for internal collaboration, social sharing, and servicing the business way beyond marketing. Content and social tools will not become more enterprise-like. Enter-prise tools will become more content and conversation enabled.

CONCLUSION
Changing Everything You Know — And Nothing You Do

"As a rock star, I have two instincts: I want to have fun, and I want to change the world. I have a chance to do both."

—Bono

Congratulations. Your journey is about to begin.

Our goal was to take you just beyond the ordinary world that you've inhabited and leave you just beyond the gates to a new road. It's one that like any epic journey is filled with tests, challenges, and ultimately, the opportunity for unprecedented success.

Bono's instincts above are not too dissimilar for content marketers. We are in an amazing environment right now. Organizational silos are coming down as we speak. We have the opportunity to not only change the workplace; we can and will change the lives of our prospects and customers … through managing the storytelling process.

You've got a few tools now — others will be coming. You have a support system to return to whenever you need — we'll be there. That's right — we're here with you. Because guess what? We're just beginning, too. We're on this journey with you.

We'll learn right alongside of you — we want to hear the success stories, the struggles, the failures along the way, and the creative insights that only YOU can bring to the table. We're serious — our contact information is at the end of this book.

This book will hopefully help to put your content marketing strategy and process into perspective; however, it's your passion and your hard work that will determine your success. In the end, tactics will change, your story will change, the Web and social media will change — but you are the constant. You will frequently change everything you know

– but you won't change what you do.

There's a wonderful story of two women — Irna Phillips and Anne Hummert — that exemplifies this. It's 1930 and the height of the Great Depression. Both women had a passion for content, and ultimately became immensely successful with that passion.

Irna came to Chicago in 1930 and broke into the new media of the time — radio. Her passion for content led her to create family dramas that were ultimately serialized on the radio. Anne, who was roughly the same age as Irna, was a fan of those serialized radio dramas and she worked for an advertising agency. She proposed the (at the time) radical idea of having companies (predominantly Procter & Gamble) sponsor these serialized dramas.

You can probably guess the end of this story — it was the birth of what we know today as soap operas. Over the 15 years that followed, Irna constantly adapted and created a number of the most popular soap operas on the radio, and ultimately created the first television soap opera *As The World Turns*. And, as for Anne, during the 1930s and 1940s, she and her team generated 50% of all daytime radio advertising revenue. Passion for content and marketing wasn't just a driver of that marketing success story – it was *the* driver of success.

Skip ahead now to 1958 and the classic McGraw-Hill *Man In The Chair* advertisement. If you're not familiar with it, it is simply a picture of a grumpy man in a chair and the copy simply says:

I don't know who you are
I don't know your company
I don't know your company's product
I don't know what your company stands for
I don't know your company's customers
I don't know your company's record
I don't know your company's reputation
Now … What was it you wanted to sell me?

Back in 2009, it was recognized as the #1 B2B advertisement of all time by the Business Marketing Association (BMA). And the presentation at the BMA event that year reminded us what the ad was all about: content as relationship — content as conversation — content as transparency — content as brand — and content as marketing.

When the BMA honored this campaign, they did a live re-enactment of The Man In The Chair — Yesterday and Today. Of course, the "yesterday" version of the "man in the chair" is a grumpy version of our grandpa — in his bow tie and "get off my lawn" attitude. But the second is our own generation's version of that — the overly busy executive with the Bluetooth Borg-attached headset trying to (in real-time, of course) research the company he's on the phone with. He checks LinkedIn, Google, and the company's Web site and seems more frustrated by lack of information rather than the scant information he does find.

Today's marketing landscape is changing everything we know about the ways to find out about a company, the way we build our tribes (as Seth Godin would say), and the tools we use to manage our relationships.

But it changes nothing we do. It's still the fundamentals that matter. Relationships. Honesty. Point of View. Differentiation. Content.

Go out and make yours remarkable.

ACKNOWLEDGMENTS

There is a wonderful quote by the travel writer Tim Cahill that says "a journey is best measured in friends rather than miles." The fast and furious journey of creating this book has been a blessing of an abundance of friends, both old and new. From the leadership and mastery of bringing this book from concept to market in (literally) four months to his continuing assistance with strategy, we want to thank Newt Barrett, president and publisher at CMI Books. If you found this book readable, it is because of the formidable talents of Lisa Murton Beets and the unbelievable care and energy she put into editing it. The beautiful design (both inside and out) and the wonderfully helpful illustrations were created by Dana Ross and Joe Watson. Another big thanks goes to Jeffery Hayzlett, for his exceptional foreword and support of this book and content marketing in general.

As well, we are humbled by the support of our friends in the content marketing community who have paved the way for this book, especially the contributors and consultants at the Content Marketing Institute. You inspire us.

Finally, we would like to thank our families (especially our patient, caring and extraordinary wives) for their support. Trust us when we say that we know not everyone is as passionate about content marketing as the two of us are. And, for pretending to care deeply as we bounced ideas, tried out new concepts and generally talked about marketing strategies — we thank you deeply for engaging in this book.

ABOUT THE AUTHORS

Robert Rose
Robert@BigBlueMoose.Net
Twitter: @Robert_Rose
About.Me/RobertRose

As the Founder and Chief Troublemaker at Big Blue Moose and the Strategist in Residence for the Content Marketing Institute, Robert helps marketers become storytellers.

A recognized expert in content marketing strategy, digital media, and the social Web, Robert innovates creative and technical strategies for a wide variety of clientele. He's helped large companies such as PTC, First American Title, Valley Crest, American Camp Association, and Nissan tell their story more effectively through the Web. He's worked to strategize digital marketing efforts for entertainment and media brands such as Dwight Yoakam, Nickelodeon, and NBC. And, he's helped marketers at smaller organizations, such as East Harlem Tutorial Program, Coburn Ventures, Hippo, and Magus to amplify their story through content marketing and social Web strategies.

Robert lives in Los Angeles, California, with his beautiful wife Elizabeth and their golden doodle Daisy.

Joe Pulizzi
joe@junta42.com
Twitter: @juntajoe
About.Me/JoePulizzi

Joe Pulizzi, known in some far-off circles as the "Godfather of Content Marketing," is a leading author, speaker, and strategist for content marketing. Joe is first and foremost a content marketing evangelist, and founded the Content Marketing Institute, which includes client-vendor matching site Junta42 as well as the premier international content marketing event Content Marketing World, the magazine *Chief Content Officer*, and the blogging service *SocialTract*. Joe is also co-author of the highly praised book *Get Content Get Customers* (Mc-Graw-Hill).

Awarded "Custom Media Innovator of the Year" by American Business Media, voted Who's Who in Media Business by *BtoB Magazine*, and recognized as the Most Influential Content Strategist via LavaCon, Joe travels around North America and Europe talking to marketers and business owners about how they are indeed publishers, and what they need to do about it.

Joe writes one of the most popular content marketing blogs in the world and is overly passionate about the color orange. He lives in Cleveland, Ohio (yes, CTOWN), with his amazing wife Pam and their two boys Joshua and Adam.

CPSIA information can be obtained at www.ICGtesting.com
Printed in the USA
BVOW040323181111

276400BV00005B/72/P

9 780983 330714